FIVE SMOOTH STONES

Our Power To Heal Without Medicine Through The Science Of Prayer

by
Janis Hunt Johnson, CS

cs renewal

...SHARING PRACTICAL TOOLS FOR HEALING
WITHOUT MEDICINE THROUGH THE SCIENCE OF PRAYER.

Published by CS Renewal, an imprint of The Wisdom Exchange
www.csrenewal.com

Printed and bound in the United States of America

Author's note: All healings described in this book are my own, or I know
of them first-hand in my circle of family and friends, unless otherwise
noted. Nothing has been fictionalized in any way whatsoever. A patient's
identity is often omitted to protect the individual's privacy.

Book, jacket, and logo design by Altemus Design
www.coroflot.com/altemusdesign

Author portrait photography by www.beyondimages.com. Hair styling
and makeup by Susan Zastoupil.

Cover photograph taken at the Labyrinth fountain, Trinity Garden, Trinity
Episcopal Church, Ashland, Oregon, by Jay Newman, Newman Images
www.newmanimages.com

Cataloging-in-Publication Data
Johnson, Janis Elisabeth Hunt, 1960–
    Five smooth stones: our power to heal without medicine through the
science of prayer / Janis Hunt Johnson.
    p. cm.
    Includes bibliographic references.
    ISBN 978-0-89411-019-1 (pbk.)
    1. Spiritual healing. 2. Healing — Practice — Handbooks, manuals,
etc. 3. Religion and science.
    I. Title.

The frontispiece is a poem entitled *The House We Dwell In*, by Martha J.
Hine, as published in *The Christian Science Sentinel*, v. 86, no. 42, p. 1776.

"We each have a sanctuary —
stone by stone —
built from our prayers."

— Martha J. Hine

This book is dedicated
to my Mom,
Marjorie E. Hunt,
who first told me to write it —
and to my Dad,
Rev. J. Richard Hunt,
who first taught me
how to answer God's call.

Contents

3 Philosophers' stone

Let's get real.

THE TRUTH ABOUT THE LIE

4 Touchstone

Let's be practical.

THE LAW OF LIFE CONQUERS DEATH

5 Capstone

Let's get radical.

Completion

Let's be discerning.

Introduction:
the act of starting something new;
an innovation.

MIND

Let's be logical.

THE BEGINNING — ONE MIND

Five Smooth Stones

Whatever your religious background may be, you're probably familiar with the Bible story of David and Goliath. Goliath was a Philistine with a large army preparing for an attack on the Israelites. He was "six cubits and a span" tall (that's over eight feet high by our modern measurements) — a menacing giant of a guy at any rate — with a great deal of armor, and a huge spear and shield. He stood at the top of a mountain shouting, trying to intimidate his foe to do battle.

When a young shepherd boy named David said he'd challenge Goliath, he rejected any armor or sword, saying, "I cannot go with these; for I have not proved them." Instead he took his shepherd's staff, "and chose him five smooth stones out of the brook, and put them in a shepherd's bag" (I Samuel 17:39, 40).

When Goliath saw this diminutive young shepherd, standing there with only a shepherd's staff to defend himself, he laughed out loud. But David stood firm.

"You come to me with a sword, and with a spear, and with a shield," David said, "but I come to you in the name of God. Today God will deliver you into my hands. And everyone will know that there is a God, and that God saves not with sword and spear: For the battle is God's, who will give you into our hands" (see I Samuel 17:45, 46).[2]

Then, against all odds, David — *expecting* to succeed — simply started out alone, running towards the entire army! And he put his hand in the bag, and took a stone and flung it, and hit that Philistine smack-dab in the middle of his forehead. And Goliath fell down dead. First try. Not bad for a kid. Saved his people with one clean blow.

I like this story, because whether historically accurate or pure legend,

I know it's true. I know that, even though I often feel like David facing Goliath, I can summarily defeat *any* problem I encounter, if I choose the right weapon.

Whenever I am challenged by any difficulty, large or small, if I stop ruminating, and recall David's faith and victory over Goliath the Philistine, I know a solution is within my grasp.

The Word

> "Continue in the things you've learned and have been assured of, knowing of whom you have learned them; and that since you were a child, you have known the holy scriptures, which are able to make you wise.... All scripture is given by inspiration of God, and is profitable for doctrine, for reproof, for correction, for instruction in righteousness: that the follower of God may be perfect, thoroughly equipped for all good works." (see II Timothy 3:14–17)

In the deluxe 1930 edition of Webster's dictionary, one of the definitions for the word *Philistine* offers a quote from English essayist Augustine Birrell (1850–1933): "By a Philistine, I suppose we mean one who lives and moves and has his being in the realm of ordinary and conventional ideas." Additional definitions say: "One regarded as antagonistic to those of artistic or poetic temperament; a prosaic person.... One temporarily inaccessible to or afraid of new ideas, especially to ideas whose acceptance would involve change; an active or passive opponent of progress or progressive ideas."

All of us have encountered at one time or another "Philistines" of various kinds attempting to bully us — people, problems, or even physical ailments — threatening to conquer us. These challengers try to keep us from knowing the truth, from growing and progressing. We've probably even heard Philistine voices in our own head! And they can be very stubborn!

Sometimes, our problems may seem a lot bigger and even more frightening than Goliath and his whole army. How do you face the seemingly insurmountable obstacles in your life that shout at you from the mountaintop, and try to make you feel small, overwhelmed, and helpless?

In contrast to Birrell's parody, the Apostle Paul wrote that "we live, and move and have our being" *in God* (Acts 17:28). If we are indeed created, constituted and governed by God, what is our role as individual expressions of God's Infinite Goodness?[3] What weapons are best for battling the evils of this world? In other words, where shall we go to choose our own "five smooth stones"?

First of all, we can take a cue from our Maker. God is All-powerful, All-knowing, and All-encompassing. God is only Good. God knows there's nothing to worry about. God knows that nothing whatsoever can cause harm. In light of all this, just for the sake of discussion (since God really doesn't require anything) what would a Divine "sword and spear" be like?

Paul points to an answer: "the word of God is quick and powerful, and sharper than any twoedged sword, piercing even to the dividing asunder of soul and spirit, and of the joints and marrow, and is a discerner of the thoughts and intents of the heart" (Hebrews 4:12). Along those same lines, the Apostle John begins his Gospel with: "In the beginning was the Word, and the Word was with God, and the Word was God" (John 1:1).

Truly, The Divine One doesn't have any need for weapons. The Word is enough.

Accordingly, faced with a challenge, my "five smooth stones" most often come from an exploration into the meaning of the Word. When I say the Word, I'm not necessarily talking about the Bible or any particular religion's sacred texts, although I myself do most frequently include them as my study tools. I'm talking about all words, and the thoughts behind them. There are a lot more meanings to words than we ordinarily realize — until we start looking deeper, where we can discover a whole realm of ideas underneath — affecting our thoughts, our emotions, and even our health, actions, and interactions with others. In the Benedictine monastic tradition, *lectio* (Latin for "reading") is the daily practice of reading small passages of scripture and then milking for meaning any word or phrase that provokes the reader's attention.[4] A reflective process, an honest self-inquiry through the exploration of words that speak to us directly can bring us to an awareness of what specifically needs to be dealt with in our lives.

In the original Greek, the term John used for "the Word" is *Logos*, meaning "reason or intelligence," either expressed outwardly in speech, or inwardly in the mind.[5] If God actually is Reason and Intelligence Itself, as John suggests, then it makes perfect sense to follow an inquiry into the inward or outward expressions of that Reason and Intelligence. God is therefore *as close as our own thought*.

Ultimately, the Word is so powerful, It can change our lives, It can make the blind to see. Not just metaphorically. I mean literally. *The Word heals*.

Because the Word is, in a real sense, already our very identity, we can discover this power and prove it for ourselves!

As we begin each day, we can put on a lot of heavy armor that the world tells us is only logical — or, we can carefully choose our five smooth stones. We have the power within us to prevail — to fight any battle and win —

against any belief that there is some *other* power *outside* of the One and Only Omnipotent Omnipresent God. Which way will we choose to go?

I think the Bible is a pretty good book. It's a guide for living — often offering practical information anyone can use. Whether the Bible is history or myth is irrelevant. I happen to think it's a bit of both. Either way, like all ancient wisdom texts, the Bible contains *spiritual truths* we can utilize daily to make our lives better and to enrich the lives of those around us.

I grew up reading the Bible, in a Protestant Christian household, the daughter of a Lutheran minister.[6] I have to admit the Bible is a major part of my personal culture. You may have grown up in a different religious tradition, or with no religion at all. But what's important here is the Word, which stands above all religions, doctrines, cultures, or time frames. There are indeed a good number of sacred texts in the world — books you may have treasured your whole life — containing words of wisdom that are meaningful and sustaining for you. If so, don't just leave them on the shelf. Embrace the ones that speak to you. Study them, guard them as your cherished guides. They can only grow more valuable as you grow.

My favorite book of all is the quintessential textbook on Mind-healing, *Science and Health with Key to the Scriptures* by Mary Baker Eddy, the founder and discoverer of Christian Science, first published in 1875. Just by reading this book I was healed of severe chronic carpal tunnel syndrome, after doctors and herbal remedies had been unable to help. Right then and there I threw out all pills and medicines of every kind, even vitamins — and I've been much healthier and happier since.[7]

Believe it or not, for me, probably the most holy of all books is a really good dictionary! That, and a good thesaurus! As you read on, you'll see what I mean.[8] I encourage you to utilize whatever brings you closer to the Word, in whatever your native tongue may be.

Being Itself

> "For whatsoever things were written aforetime were written
> for our learning, that we through patience and comfort of the
> scriptures might have hope." (Romans 15:4)

With *Five Smooth Stones* I share with you my own journey of discovery — into what we are, what we can accomplish, and how we can improve our lives and the lives of others. I humbly join with anyone seeking truth, and it is my wish that together in this process we will leave behind any bias — religious, doctrinal, or otherwise.

Let's resolve to set aside the Philistine "realm of ordinary and conventional ideas" — without fear, and with a willingness simply to entertain some new ideas. At least for a time, let new insights settle in and stay a while. Each new point in your understanding may be another smooth stone you'll want to add to your bag.

Here we can start with pure theology. *Theology*, taken literally from the Greek, means "The Word of God," and is not bound to any specific religious practice.

In the Bible story of Moses' meeting with God, when Moses asked for God's name, God replied, "I Am That I Am" (Exodus 3:14). In Hebrew, the phrase is *Ehyeh-Asher-Ehyeh*, which can also be interpreted as "I Am Who I Am," or "I Will Be What I Will Be." Some scholars even think that God was using a play on words, to say: "I am Being Itself; there is actually no word to describe Me."

Let's look at this exciting possibility. That God is Being Itself! God isn't only a noun. As Rabbi David Cooper says, God is a Verb.[9] God is all-embracing, all-encompassing, the center and circumference of all Being.[10]

In the Jewish tradition, God's name is too sacred to be uttered, but many names have been used over the centuries by rabbis, including *Memra* (Aramaic for "The Word") and what the Kabbalists called *Ein-Sof* ("The Infinite"). In Islam, there are ninety-nine beautiful names for God (*Allah*), who, as The Prophet Muhammad declared, is One.[11]

All this talk of God may make some people uncomfortable. For many of us, in our religious upbringing (or lack thereof), there has persisted the mythological notion that God is high and mighty, while we are lowly and clueless — even sinful. Generally the story goes that most of the time we wander around in the dark, bumping into the roadblocks and mysteries of life, while God, The Big Guy, sits on some King's throne somewhere, capriciously arranging things for His own amusement — still Zeus on some Mount Olympus. Most of us would rather choose to be an agnostic or atheist than acknowledge a God like that.

But let's assume that God is not humanoid. God is not a person, place or thing. *God is not corporeal.* None of us can see God physically with material eyes. God is not male or female, but expresses both qualities — as well as an infinite number of other Divine characteristics, which we are here to investigate. And God certainly isn't confined to any particular planet, but spans the entire universe, which most likely, physicists tell us, includes perhaps an infinite number of planes of existence as well.

So God doesn't much care about what religion you are or aren't. The Divine One is beyond all human opinions, and doesn't leave out any of us.[12]

It shouldn't seem so surprising that actually, the best thing you can do in any crisis — or even in an everyday situation that rubs you the wrong way — is to turn to God. Try making prayer your *first* resort, instead of your last, and you'll see what I mean.

Prayer is a listening process. We don't necessarily have to do any talking. In fact, this is a good time to cultivate silence. God already knows all, and therefore knows us through and through. God gives us the answer as soon as we are quiet. As an ancient song says, "Be still, and know that I am God" (Psalm 46:10). No more opinions. No more preconceived notions. No more desperation. No more complaining. No more ruminating. No more clanking armor weighing us down. Listen. God is right here. Now. Telling us the truth.

Because all questions have been answered in The Infinite — whether mundane or complicated — once we are quiet and still, listening, seeking guidance, the answers we need will be provided to us. From what task to cancel in your overbooked day, to how to respond when someone points a gun at you, God *will* tell you the best course of action.

Anatomy Lessons

> "We are at liberty to change our belief of things as often as we get new light. We should not let our vanity compel us to adhere to a proposition simply because we have taken a stand thereon. We should be willing to relinquish our former views and change our thought on any subject as often as wisdom furnishes us enlightenment.... Is a general less fit to lead his army because in the heat of battle he changes his tactics under the guidance of wisdom?.... [We] are minutemen, armed and equipped to respond to any call of wisdom, always ready and willing to abandon personal views or opinions, and to allow that Mind to be in [us] 'which was also in Christ Jesus [see Philippians 2:5].'"[13]

If God is incorporeal, and God is All, then logically it follows that *man must also be incorporeal.* God is Mind. And *we are God's thoughts.*

Before we go any further, I want to explain the real meaning behind the word *man.* For most of my life, the use of this word often troubled me, because it seems to leave out half of humanity. Yet now whenever I come across the word *man* or *mankind,* I can instantly redeem the meaning by recalling the true definition: The word *man* actually goes back to the Sanskrit, *manu* and *manas,* meaning "mind."[14] (The word *mantra* also comes from the same root, *manyate,* "one who thinks.") You can't get any clearer than that!

If man is incorporeal, what is matter? Matter is a human concept based on the supposed evidence of the five senses. The very existence of matter, over the last hundred years or so, has been disproved (or at least seriously called into question) by many reputable physicists, even as I write this.

Even if you don't know anything about physics, you already know from your own experience that your senses can play tricks on you. A branch will look crooked at the water's surface when placed in a stream. The earth seems flat at the horizon, our sun "rising" and "setting" — yet we know we are actually on a spherical planet spinning in space at an incredible speed around a star. The Doppler effect makes the sound of a passing train sound different up close and far away. If you take a few minutes, I'm sure you can think of many other examples.

Because science has been long dominated by materialism, most of us were taught in school that everything is mindless matter, and that matter is made up of atoms — protons, neutrons, and electrons. But quantum physics tells us that matter is divisible further still, made up of other particles with fanciful names like WIMPS, zinos, leptons, gluons, and quarks, and even "virtual particles," which are not directly detectable but have measurable effects. Murray Gell-Mann, the scientist who coined the term quark from a passage in James Joyce's novel *Finnegan's Wake*, admits *quarks* are merely "mathematical entities."[15] Physicist Paul Davies explains that the subatomic world is populated by all sorts of "strange objects" which we call "particles," but "[w]hat they really are, we do not know."[16]

Throughout this book I will bring out such examples from scientific inquiry to underscore that, at the very least: Due to overwhelming evidence, physicists nowadays must admit (many still unwillingly) that the nature of reality is not what we once thought it was. That means a whole new world of possibilities is now open to us.

We are living in the midst of a paradigm shift in thought, and its inevitable conclusion is the end of materialism. Discussing this issue at length in their book, *The Matter Myth*, physicists Paul Davies and John Gribbin observe: "However certain we are that our present picture describes how the [u]niverse *actually* is, we cannot rule out the possibility that some new and better way of looking at things, utterly unimaginable to us now, will be discovered in the future."[17]

Scientists also admit that there must be more than three dimensions, probably at least eleven in total, and perhaps more — so there is much more than only what we can see, hear, smell, taste, and touch. Particles have been shown in the laboratory to seem to behave on their own, in defiance of conventional time and space constraints. And the strange thing is, experiments have repeatedly shown that an electron is both a particle and a wave. Not only that, it is actually "there" and "known" only when an observer is measuring it. Thus the nature of quantum reality shows that *nothing is real unless it is observed.*[18] When it comes right down to it, if matter can be broken down into molecules, atoms, and then into smaller and smaller particles ad infinitum — then, any way you look at it, there's really *nothing* left.

Even if we don't fully comprehend or accept quantum physics, we may be willing to admit that at least there is some doubt as to what constitutes "reality." So in this vast conundrum of inexplicable particles and/or nothingness, where does that leave us? Back at the basic premise — that All is Mind. Peter E. Hodgson, Head of the Nuclear Physics Theoretical Group at the Nuclear Physics Laboratory at Oxford University, once asked himself why all hydrogen atoms are the same: "They must be connected in some way, by a mind that designed and made them."[19] In 1969, physicist and Nobel Prize–winner Erwin Shrödinger asserted even more succinctly: "in truth there is only one mind."[20]

In 1971, Apollo Astronaut Dr. Edgar Mitchell took a trip to the moon and back. As he viewed the Earth suspended as a sphere in the vastness of space, he experienced what he described as "a grand epiphany," and his life "was irrevocably altered":

> What I experienced during that three-day trip home was nothing short of an overwhelming sense of universal *connectedness*. I actually felt what has been described as an ecstasy of unity.... And there was the sense that our presence as space travelers, and the existence of the universe itself, was not accidental but that there was an intelligent process at work. I perceived the universe as in some way conscious.[21]

If, as these accomplished scientists suggest, there is only One Mind, how does the knowledge of this Divine Science affect us? Mary Baker Eddy, the healer[22] who (re)discovered this Science back in 1866, wrote: "Divine Science, rising above physical theories, excludes matter, resolves *things* into *thoughts*, and replaces material sense with spiritual ideas."[23]

But if we are ideas and not physical bodies, then are we mere gossamer — intangible, fleeting, lacking identity or purpose? On the contrary, our individuality is no less tangible because it is spiritual (i.e., incorporeal) instead of material. In fact, *if* things *are* thoughts, and we aren't at the mercy of matter after all, then this understanding of our spiritual individuality makes each of us *more* real, giving us a truly formidable strength to be reckoned with, and thus enabling us to conquer any evil.[24]

Isn't thought tangible? When you dream, isn't a table just as solid? A car just as fast? A kiss just as tender?

Dreams may be stories our so-called human subconscious uses to solve problems in our waking hours. But let's take that idea further: Our reality is a story of our own choosing. What we are conscious *of* is what *comes into* consciousness. A couple of quick examples: If you decide not to smoke, doesn't smoking eventually fade from your experience? If you have a toothache, and you watch a hilarious movie, during that time don't you forget your affliction? What possibilities does this suggest?

What we've long considered to be our physical body, knowable through the five senses, is actually *instead a manifestation of our thought*. Deepak Chopra, MD, a pioneer in the exploration of the mind-body connection, says that literally "a person's body is nothing but an expression of all the ideas [the person has] about it."[25] When we can understand this, then our bodies, our identities, become *more* substantial, not less. When we know that matter and so-called physical laws hold no power over us after all, we are then graced with the power of *the universal law* — to heal any problem whatsoever — *by adjusting our thought*.

Many great thinkers have put forth, in various ways, this same liberating concept, including The Buddha, who said simply: "we are what we think."[26] Astavakra, the eminent Hindu teacher and Advaita Vedanta philosopher (c. 100–300 CE), agreed:

If you think you are free,
You are free.

If you think you are bound,
You are bound.

For the saying is true:
You are what you think.[27]

Admittedly the notion that thought is paramount isn't new. From 17th-century French mathematician and philosopher René Descartes, who uttered the phrase "I think, therefore I exist," and back to Greek philosopher Plato (c. 427–c. 348 BC), who searched for unity behind the changing sensations of the visible universe, we have been seeking ways to explain consciousness.[28]

Now that modern science is reuniting with philosophy, slowly admitting that there is no conflict after all between the rationality of science and the once so-called foolhardiness of faith, we are headed towards a time of awakening — when we can be fully conscious of who we truly are, and what always has existed. If we become conscious for just one moment of the fact that, because there is only Mind, each of us is an idea *inseparable* from the One Divine Consciousness, then absolutely anything *is* possible.

When we are suffering, if we rise above the specious material circumstances to the higher spiritual truth, we can see in reality that we are already rescued, already healed, already saved from heartache, danger, or sorrow. God, The Absolute, puts forth, and allows in, only good. Thus if we align our thought with God's, our mistaken acceptance of the problem will dissolve — disappearing into the nothingness from whence it came.

I want to make it very clear that *this book is not in any way about healing our lives through the human mind.* Willpower on our part is hubris — our own ego trying to make something happen. Maintaining our own willpower is a *denial* that there is a Higher Power, because we are declaring that there can be *more* than Infinite All, *more* than The One I Am. An arrogance on our part — asserting that each of us even *has* an individual human mind (ego) in the first place that could possibly *be* separate from the One Ego — causes only strife. It is by *yielding* to the One Mind that we experience permanent healing.

How can this yielding process be explained? If it is *not faith* healing (human-mind willpower), but rather healing through an *understanding* of reality (Mind power), then it must be scientific — which means it can be tested, demonstrated, learned, and practiced.

If we go back to look at the nature of electrons (acting as both waves and particles), this key aspect shows us that a particle of light visits all points along its path at the same moment, so there's *no distance* at all to cross the entire universe in an instant. This unified description of spacetime explains many physical phenomena, and is already "the accepted view of the physical world" for a growing number of scientists, according to physicists Davies and Gribbin.[29]

Although many scientists are still ready to argue the point, Larry Dossey, MD, a physician of internal medicine and author of many books on prayer and healing, would agree. Dossey suggests that what physicists call the "nonlocality" of particles is the key to understanding consciousness. For me, the wave/particle paradox points to the unity/individual paradox. As Dossey further contends, prayer works over great distances because in actuality *there's no distance to cover.*[30] He comments on the controversy that persists in the medical and scientific communities, even in the face of convincing evidence: "the struggle over [the] nonlocal mind is often not a debate about actual evidence but a battle fought by the ego to maintain its sense of importance."[31]

Sooner or later, we will have to come to terms with what quantum nonlocality teaches: Even widely separated particles cannot be considered independent entities.[32] If this is so, says Dossey, then "[n]ot only does this nonlocal view of consciousness connect us with The Absolute, it unites us with each other."[33] What a blessing and a comfort that is — to see clearly that faith in prayer to heal one another (even over thousands of miles) is scientifically logical, and therefore can be proven and made practical!

Nonetheless, here's how it goes most of the time nowadays, in a world still based on the premise that everything is made up of matter. When you are suffering from an ailment, a medical doctor, trained in conventional anatomy and pathology, believing that you are a physical being, examines all the evidence available to the five senses, inspects your nooks and crannies, and comes up with a diagnosis. The physician prescribes a drug, regimen, or activity that may or may not cure the belief you and the doctor both now have that there is a problem in a material body.

But if we look instead to the realm of Divine Science, on the other hand, where we recognize that All is Mind, then *anatomy*, as Eddy puts it, is defined as "mental self-knowledge, and consists in the dissection of thoughts to discover their quality, quantity, and origin."[34] The word *diagnosis* is Greek for "to know through" or "to distinguish." So, what, then, is the metaphysician's diagnosis? We ask: What does God know? — only wholeness, only unity, only health, only harmony. God's diagnosis, knowing us through and through, is that *all is well*. A clean bill of health for all eternity. The Divine Mind thus distinguishes *the false supposition* of material discord from *the actual fact* that each of us has an uninterrupted alignment with the Divine — throwing out any disturbances as irrelevant. When we eliminate mistaken thoughts, right thoughts abide, and we are healed. This expert diagnosis, a thorough distinguishing between the real and the unreal, is true understanding — an understanding that heals.[35]

So is it really possible to gain this elevated understanding? *Understanding* has the same literal meaning as *substance*, i.e., "to stand under," from the Latin. Is our very substance — our essence, our underlying reality, our *understanding* — material or spiritual? When you know and prove the truth for yourself — that you are indeed an expression of Mind only — you will see that your rightful self is forever free of disease.

Why should we accept the common-view law, based in matter, that says viruses and other microscopic activities cause disease? Outdated human theories make the same mistake about a supposed mind (long believed to be located in the brain)[36] residing in a supposed body that 2nd-century astronomer Ptolemy made regarding the solar system. But his postulation, accepted for centuries — that the planets and sun revolved around the earth — didn't change the fact, to be uncovered eventually by Polish astronomer Copernicus some 1,400 years later, that the earth actually revolves around the sun.

And just as modern astronomy has debunked the ancient belief that celestial bodies influence our lives, Divine Science corrects the errors regarding our terrestrial bodies — revealing our true identity as Mind's reflection.[37] Thus, the microscopic world of bacteria, viruses, diseases, and germs has no more power over our lives than the macroscopic world of the stars does. So bodies either "in here" or "out there" are both erroneous notions of a power apart from the One Mind.

We as individuals are not bodies, each with a separate mind or soul inside. Instead, each individual is a unique idea, emanating from and inseparable from the One Mind. We must let go of any notion of an isolated human mind or self, which is only a supposition of a separate ego that doesn't really exist.[38] There can be no separation of the One Mind from Its thoughts. There is only One Self — and each of us is a complete and unique facet of that One. Centuries ago, Astavakra echoed this view:

> Child,
> If you wish to be free
> Shun the poison of the senses.
>
> Seek the nectar of truth,
> Of love and forgiveness,
> Simplicity and happiness.
>
> Earth, fire and water,
> The wind and the sky —
> You are none of these.
>
> If you wish to be free,
> Know you are the Self,
> The witness of all these,
> The heart of awareness.
> Set your body aside.
> Sit in your own awareness.
>
> You will at once be happy,
> Forever still,
> Forever free.[39]

Reflection

"Understanding is a wellspring of life for anyone who has it."
(Proverbs 16:22)

If you look at the calm surface of a lake, and see a tree reflected in the water, you don't have to look up to know that the tree is there. When you stand in front of a mirror, do you doubt your own existence? On the contrary, you are assured of your presence, able to see how that new haircut really looks good on you. If you lift your arm, the image in the mirror does likewise.

Now compare yourself at the mirror to your Divine Principle, God. Call the mirror Divine Science, and call your real self Its reflection.[40] See how true the reflection is to the Original. As the image of yourself appears in a mirror, so you are a reflection of God. Since God is perfection, wholeness and freedom, so are you. You can't be otherwise.

When everything around you seems to be turmoil and struggle, and troubles loom on every horizon, stop. Be still. Be quiet. Like the calm surface of a lake. Think clearly. In a word: Reflect. Meditate, don't ruminate. *Reflect*, don't analyze. An analysis of the problem will get you nowhere, merely leading you into more misery and confusion, down into the mire of material existence, which is always chaotic.

But if you are reflecting The Absolute, you are listening for Divine thoughts. You are turning back towards that Divine Mirror to see your own reflection in the glass. Re-Mind yourself of your true identity!

The Apostle Paul, writing in the year 55 CE to early Christians in Corinth, spoke of seeing ourselves through "a glass, darkly," like "a poor reflection as in a mirror; then we shall see face to face... then shall I know fully, even as I am fully known" (see I Corinthians 13:12, the New International version of the Bible [NIV]). In a followup letter to Corinth that same year, he expounded on this concept: "we all, with open face beholding as in a glass the glory of The Lord, are changed into the same image from glory to glory" (II Corinthians 3:18). (It is interesting to note here that Paul's reference to "The Lord" was not to the man Jesus; the Greek word he used was *kurios*, from kuros, meaning "supremacy," or "God.") One interpretation of this verse could be: "Anyone who looks steadily, day after day, at infinite divine perfection, will be transformed into its likeness."[41]

James, an early leader of Jesus' followers in Jerusalem, living at about the same time, wrote (c. 48 CE): "Anyone who listens to the word but doesn't do what it says, is like a man who looks at his face in a mirror and, after looking at himself, goes away and immediately forgets what he looks like" (James 1:23–24, NIV). Look squarely in the Mirror. *Understand* the reality of any situation in your experience. *Distinguish* between what is true and what isn't. Go back — to your authentic self, the only true individual that ever was, is and shall be: You are a wonderful, complete, intact, unique expression of God's Allness. Throw out the other noise. It is only an untrue story — something you or someone else made up about you — so you don't need to accept it. God doesn't accept it, so you don't have to either.

How can we know what Divine thoughts are? Here's what James suggested: "The wisdom that is from above is first pure, then peaceful, gentle and easy to be entreated, full of mercy and good fruits, without partiality and without hypocrisy" (James 3:17).

To practice seeing our reflection, we must go back to what we've learned about metaphysical anatomy. In order to judge a thought, we need to see where it originates. Does it come from mistaken thinking, based on the fickleness of materiality? From the opinion of another person, which we have unconsciously accepted? From common world perceptions, which we have adopted through conditioning? Or is it from God — from Being Itself?

This reflecting process may seem like a tall order. But you can learn for yourself — and prove — what it is to reflect God. You *already have* all the Intelligence you need to understand the truth. At this very moment, you are already reflecting God, and you always will be. Truth is already revealed; all you need to do you is practice it.[42]

By now you may be saying, "This is all well and good, but last time I checked I still live in the 'real world,' where tragedy and sorrow seem to rule all around me. What good is all this pie-in-the-sky metaphysical stuff if it doesn't really apply to what I'm going through?" I would answer that I know from my own experience that Divine Science is fundamentally practical — applicable in demonstrable ways, in all times and in all places. Every day I learn this a little bit more and, even with setbacks, I continue to grow in my understanding.

One woman with a great deal of spiritual understanding nevertheless found herself suffering from cancer. Out walking one night in despair, she turned to God once more in prayer, wondering how many days she had left to live. Standing on a bridge looking down at the water, she saw the moon shining on the still surface. She suddenly recognized the fact that the moon was there — even though she was looking only at its reflection, not up to the sky. She was sure of the moon's existence because she saw its reflection. This sudden insight, applied to her own identity as God's perfect image, brought complete and permanent healing.[43]

Wherever each of us is on our own journey, we are always poised to learn more. Our individual capacity for progress and healing is infinite. After all, each of us is a reflection of The Infinite Itself! Looking at it from the rich perspective of the Hindu philosophy of Advaita Vedanta, our true identity could be summed up this way: "the impersonal Absolute," or "all-pervading Spirit" is "the essence, the Self... of all beings," called *Brahman*. *Brahman* is "that which alone is real," the "eternal principle," and which in Sanskrit means "growth" or "expansion."[44]

Like anything else of value, the Science of God must be learned and practiced in order to be made useful. Even if we know that all is Mind — and matter doesn't exist — for now we still have to get up in the morning, pay bills, mow the lawn, and so forth. So if any of this is going to make any real difference, we must prove it for ourselves, in our own experience.

I myself have experienced healing, through scientific prayer alone (all without medicine or other material remedy), of numerous conditions such as: allergies, migraine headaches, colds, burns, flu, heartburn, astigmatism (along with improved eyesight), marriage crises, financial woes, panic attacks, chest pains, even a breast lump. My scientific prayers have also healed others who can attest to prayer's effectiveness in the treatment of colic, croup, colds, pinkeye, gout, rashes, sore throat, fever, injuries, bipolar disorder, drug addiction, anxiety, heart trouble, thyroid trouble, back trouble, etc. Even computers, VCRs, cars, hurricanes, and fires can be transformed through prayer! I refer above only to those healings which I have experienced myself or have known within my own family or circle of friends. Among these, countless healings have been virtually instantaneous, or have taken place within just a few minutes or hours. You name it — whatever your difficulty, it can be healed through prayer.[45]

Why? In the next chapters we'll look at the Divine laws that govern the universe. You'll see how you can apply these laws in practical ways that make sense in your everyday life to bring healing — for yourself, and for everyone whom your life touches.

At the end of this chapter is a list of synonyms for Mind, words I sometimes like to turn to when praying, to help unblock negative thinking and generate new ways of seeing the true spiritual nature of myself or of someone else. Since God is Mind, and we are Mind's ideas, then here in this list are some Divine qualities — attributes which can be applied to describe each of us when we want to spiritualize our thought in a particular situation.

Mary Baker Eddy defines God as follows: "God is incorporeal, divine, supreme, infinite *Mind, Spirit, Soul, Principle, Life, Truth, Love*."[46] Because I've found these synonyms to be spiritually sound and practical, I have arranged this book into seven chapters to reflect these seven synonyms for God.

As we go along, I hope you'll be inspired to explore more ways to utilize the synonyms for God as tools for healing. Blank pages are available at the end of each chapter so you can add your own observations.

A thesaurus, a dictionary, the scriptures, and thou!...

MIND

behold

equipped

wit

purity

function

intelligence

mentality

disposition

SPIRIT

tone

attention

belief

sentiment

persuasion

think

observe

remark

recall

enjoy

retain

contemplate

intellect

inclination

faculty

power

conscious

lucidity

clarity

temperament

character

cognizance

conviction

view

remember

note

regard

see

recollect

revive

retrospect

remind	willing
perceive	look
watch	attend
tend	care (for)
obey	comply
follow	keep
ready	discipline
govern	aware
alive	au courant
awake	knowing
sensible	conversant
thoughtful	heedful
observant	vigilant
alert	watchful
completed	take in
astute	capacity
reasonable	wise
plan	learned
understand	resolve
reminisce	apply oneself

THESE BLANK PAGES FOR YOUR NOTES AND
PRAYERS

ENDNOTES

THE BEGINNING — ONE MIND

1   From *Don Juan,* Canto III, Stanza 88, by George Gordon Noel Byron.

2   In this book, whenever I quote verbatim from the Bible, I am citing the King James Version unless otherwise noted. I have made every effort in my writing to modernize language, and to eliminate sexism, including all references to God as "He" — since God is not anthropomorphic. Therefore, I indicate any scriptural *paraphrases* as follows: (see [Chapter: verse]). The *verbatim* quotes from the King James Bible are simply listed parenthetically as: ([Chapter:verse]). Any other translations of the Bible are also indicated parenthetically.

3   See *Science and Health with Key to the Scriptures,* by Mary Baker Eddy. Boston: The First Church of Christ, Scientist, 1875, p. 316:20–21.*

* A note about all references to or citations from *Science and Health with Key to the Scriptures* (hereinafter referred to as *S&H*) or from any of Eddy's writings: Each page of Eddy's writings has line numbers printed in the margins. Therefore, whenever I refer to a page number from any of her works, it is followed by a colon with the line number(s), to make it easier for the reader to locate that particular passage. If only one line number is given, begin reading at the first sentence starting on that line, and continue to the end of that paragraph (even if the paragraph continues on to the next page).

4   *Illuminated Life: Monastic Wisdom for Seekers of Light,* by Joan Chittister. Maryknoll, NY: Orbis Books, 2000, p. 76. Hereinafter referred to as *Illuminated Life.*

5   See *A Commentary on The Holy Bible,* Ed. by The Rev. J. R. Dummelow. New York: Macmillan, 1973 (hereinafter referred to as Dummelow), p. 774 (paraphrased):

> *Logos* — Two meanings in Greek: 1) reason or intelligence, expressed outwardly in speech; 2) reason or intelligence, expressed inwardly in the mind. Nothing is so close to us as our own thought. It is within, and is, in a very real sense, our identity, the self.

Also see *The New Strong's Exhaustive Concordance of the Bible, Comfort Print*™ *Edition,* by James Strong, LLD, STD. London and Nashville: Thomas

Nelson Publishers, 1995 (hereinafter referred to as *Strong's*), p. 54 of the *New Strong's™ Concise Dictionary of the Words in the Greek Testament with Their Renderings in the King James Version* (paraphrased):

> *Logos*— Additional meanings in Greek: something said, including the thought; The Divine Expression, i.e., the Christ.

6   My Dad is Rev. John Richard Hunt, Evangelical Lutheran Church in America (ELCA), now retired.

7   Mary Baker Eddy has already written it all better than I can. Throughout this book I am sharing the same concepts presented by Eddy, from my own individual perspective. But the substance, a universal wisdom, remains the same: There is a universal law of Divine Science for healing. In 1896, Eddy wrote that this "Science of God..., named in this century Christian Science, is leavening the lump of human thought, until the whole shall be leavened and all materialism disappear" (*Miscellaneous Writings 1883–1896* by Mary Baker Eddy. Boston: The Christian Science Publishing Society, 1896, p. 166:23–26. Hereinafter referred to as *Miscellaneous Writings.*)

8   For a fun and practical study on the spirituality of words, read *God's Dictionary: Divine Definitions for Everyday Enlightenment* by Susan Corso. New York: Jeremy P. Tarcher/Putnam, 2002.

9   See *God is a Verb: Kabbalah and the Practice of Mystical Judaism,* by David A. Cooper. New York: Riverhead Books, 1997.

10   See *S&H,* p. 203:32–1.

11   See *The Oxford Dictionary of World Religions,* Ed. by John Bowker. Oxford and New York: Oxford University Press, 1997 (hereinafter referred to as *World Religions*), p. 48, 379, and 701. Background help on the Hebrew came from my friend, novelist David Richard Walter. For a good basic introduction to Islam, I recommend the booklet entitled *Islam Is...* by Pete Seda. Ashland, OR: Al-Haramain Islamic Foundation Inc., 2002.

12   See *S&H,* p. 192:6–10.

13   *God's Law of Adjustment,* by Adam H. Dickey. Boston: Christian Science Publishing Society, p. 15–16, 1971.

14   See *S&H* p. 525:7–16 for additional shades of meaning for the word *man* from Saxon, Welsh, Hebrew, and Icelandic.

15   *The Search for Superstrings, Symmetry, and the Theory of Everything,* by John

Gribbin. New York: Little, Brown, 1999 (hereinafter referred to as *Search for Superstrings*), p. 93.

16 *Search for Superstrings*, p. 51.

17 *The Matter Myth: Dramatic Discoveries that Challenge Our Understanding of Physical Reality*, by Paul Davies and John Gribbin. New York: Simon & Schuster/Touchstone, 1992 (hereinafter referred to as *Matter Myth*), p. 20.

18 *Search for Superstrings*, p. 153.

19 *Spiritual Evolution: Scientists Discuss Their Beliefs*, Ed. by John Marks Templeton and Kenneth Seeman Giniger. New York: The K. S. Giniger Co. & London and Philadelphia: Templeton Foundation Press, 1998 (hereinafter referred to as *Spiritual Evolution*), p. 58.

20 *Spiritual Evolution*, p. 35.

21 *The Way of the Explorer: An Apollo Astronaut's Journey Through the Material and Mystical Worlds*, by Dr. Edgar D. Mitchell, with Dwight Arnan Williams. New York: G. P. Putnam's Sons, 1996, p. 3–4.

22 *Note:* The second definition of the word *healer*, as defined in Webster's dictionary, is "Christian Science practitioner." Throughout this book, unless I qualify it otherwise, this is how I am applying the word.

23 *S&H*, p. 123:12–15.

24 See *S&H*, p. 269:14–20 and p. 317:16–20.

25 *Magical Mind, Magical Body*, a set of compact disc recordings of lectures by Deepak Chopra. Niles, IL: Nightingale-Conant Corporation, 1995. Hereinafter referred to as *Magical Mind, Magical Body*.

26 See *The Holographic Universe*, by Michael Talbot. New York: HarperCollins Publishers, 1991 (hereinafter referred to as *Holographic Universe*), p. 222. Talbot discusses at length the nature of thought to reality in light of quantum physics. See especially p. 138 and p. 220–222.

27 *The Heart of Awareness: A Translation of the Ashtavakra Gita*, by Thomas Byrom, foreword by J. L. Brockington. Boston: Shambhala Publications, 1990 (hereinafter referred to as *Heart of Awareness*), p. 3.

28 For a starter list of further study sources on these philosophers, see *Benét's Reader's Encyclopedia*, Fourth Edition, Ed. by Bruce Murphy. New York:

HarperCollins, 1996 (hereinafter referred to as *Reader's Encyclopedia*), p. 267 and 810.

29 See *Matter Myth,* p. 82–83.

30 *Reinventing Medicine: Beyond Mind-Body to a New Era of Healing,* by Larry Dossey, MD. San Francisco: HarperSanFrancisco, 1999 (hereinafter referred to as *Reinventing Medicine*), p. 27.

31 *Reinventing Medicine,* p. 29.

32 *Matter Myth,* p. 235.

33 *Spiritual Evolution,* p. 34. See also *Myths, Models and Paradigms: A Comparative Study in Science and Religion* by Ian G. Barbour. New York: Harper & Row, 1974.

34 *S&H,* p. 462:20–22.

35 See *S&H,* p. 505:21–22.

36 Many physicists today tell us that the human mind is not located in the brain, including Nick Herbert (author of *Quantum Reality: Beyond the New Physics,* as well as *Faster Than Light,* and *Elemental Mind*) and Peter Russell (author of *The Global Brain,* as well as *Waking Up in Time,* and *From Science to God: The Mystery of Consciousness and the Meaning of Light*). We'll consider this further in the chapter on the Law of Spirit.

37 See *S&H,* p. 122:29–6.

38 See *S&H,* p. xi:1–21.

39 *Heart of Awareness,* p. 1.

40 See *S&H,* p. 515:25–4.

41 "A New Year's Wish," *The Christian Science Monitor,* January 1–2, 2003, p. 19. [No author's name given]

42 See *S&H,* p. 174:20–21.

43 For the whole story see "Disease Statistics — Or The Power Of Divine Law?" by Corinne Jane Teeter, in *The Christian Science Journal,* v. 114, no. 3, March 1996, p. 19–21.

44 See *World Religions,* p. 17 and 163.

45   *An important note:* All healings described in this book are my own, or I know of them first-hand in my circle of family and friends, unless otherwise noted. A patient's identity is often omitted to protect the individual's privacy.

46   *S&H,* p. 465:9 (italics mine).

1

Cornerstone:
something of fundamental importance;
a basic element; foundation.

PRINCIPLE

Let's be rational.

> "[God says] I will put my laws
> into their mind,
> and write them
> in their hearts;
> I will put my law
> in their inward parts
> and write it in their hearts"
> (Hebrews 8:10; Jeremiah 31:33)

THE LAW OF PRINCIPLE
OBLITERATES AIMLESSNESS

What Is God?

If you look up the word *God* in the dictionary, with a little digging you'll find that along with the expected definitions, such as "a supreme being," the origin of the word itself is simply "good" — from the Swedish and Danish *god*, or German *gut*, etc. So just in case the idea of God is too far-fetched, we all recognize that there is a bit of goodness around here, at least part of the time. So let's just admit that we know *Good* exists.

For The Skeptic In All Of Us

For the sake of argument, let's look at the conventional choices we have regarding what is normally referred to as God, Deity, or the Supreme Being:

1. <u>Materialism</u>:

God doesn't exist. There's simply a material universe playing itself out at random — and that's it.

2. <u>Dualism</u>:

God exists, sure — but there's also another power, evil, so everything's screwed up because these two powers are constantly battling. In fact, often it appears evil is winning.

For decades, I wrestled with these two choices. More often than not, like many people, I straddled the fence as an agnostic, simply admitting, "I don't know." (The word *agnostic* comes from the Greek, literally meaning "unknown" or "unknowable.") But eventually I stumbled upon a third possibility:

3. Divine Science (or, The Science of Being):

God exists, and God is All. Therefore the *only* power that exists is All Good. Since you can't have *more* than all, that makes evil only an *assumption* that something else *could possibly exist outside of* Infinity. In other words, *there is no duality*. Logically, rationally, duality just can't be. Evil is simply *a mistake*. This Principle of One shows that evil, without a belief in it to prop it up, is simply a lie — supposition, smoke and mirrors, impotence, trickery.

When I say evil isn't real, I'm not discounting the world's suffering. I'm talking about evil's *counterfeit* nature. Evil isn't genuine. Evil is powerless. Evil is deceit itself. Evil has only the power it derives from anyone giving it permission to exist. Whenever we accept evil as inevitable, invite it in, and entertain it, we give it power. Evil is then insurmountable. But when wholly dismissed for what it is — an error in our thinking — evil is utterly powerless. Thus evil is self-destroyed in the presence of Truth and Love.[1]

In this scenario we are starting from Idealism, which says: all is Mind, there is only Consciousness; therefore the so-called physical world is an illusion. The Hindu name for this lie is *maya* (Sanskrit for "illusion," "cosmic delusion," "deceit," or "ignorance"). Jesus called it "the devil" or "Satan," "a liar and the father of it" (see John 8:44) — the Jewish concept of an *adversary*, which is always negated in the presence of God.

There is only one reality; it's our choice whether we decide to wake up to it, or to stay asleep. To see this reality is not to deny logic or to disengage from life. Quite the opposite. Spirituality is not an escape from the world, but a process of transforming it.[2] I'm maintaining that there is one reality — and that it is all Good, and *any* time we choose, we can see it, be it, know it. This act alone heals any circumstance. I'm going *beyond* panpsychism or pantheism — both views which say that mind and matter are intertwined, and that every particle of it all is either sentient and/or divine.[3] In an Infinite Oneness, there is not a multiplicity of consciousnesses — many individual minds warring against one another. Nor does consciousness emanate *from* matter. In the Science of Being, that just wouldn't wash. There's a larger picture here: God is Supreme Being, i.e., not *a* being, but Beingness Itself.

Thus it is reasonable and rational to conclude that matter isn't alive. In line with modern physics, we've established that matter doesn't even exist. Spirit (Mind) is Life Itself. There is One Spirit. One Life. One Principle. One Only. None else. We are all one. I'm not waxing philosophic here. I mean this literally. The connection among us all is infinite and inseverable: All is One.

Matter isn't real, but that doesn't mean that we are just blobs, or clouds of vapor drifting through oblivion without form or identity. Spirit, Mind, is as solid and as tangible as we presently think "physical reality" is. Sooner or later all scientists will come to the inevitable conclusion that what we now call matter *is* consciousness. As I touched on in the chapter on Mind, really what makes anything "solid" is simply our own conviction.

God is Principle. In Divine Science, it is a provable fact that there is a Principle governing the universe, including our own experience. Principle and Its idea is One — omnipotent, omniscient, and omnipresent.[4] This means we don't have to wander around in the dark. We are guided by Principle because It is our very Source and essence.

What is Principle?

Our word *principle* comes from the Latin *principium* meaning "beginning." We usually think of a principle as a fundamental law or rule. The dictionary adds that principle can also mean "origin" or "primary source."

How can we recognize and apply Principle to our daily challenges? Let's explore more deeply what it means to say that God is Principle. If we begin with the fact that Absolute Good is our origin and primary source — instead of starting with the mistaken notion that evil is real and that we have sprung from it — then our whole outlook changes. Remember, there's One Reality, not two. With this realization, we are *starting at the top,* every time, instead of consulting God later on as an afterthought. This is *scientific prayer* — prayer based on Principle — which is systematic and demonstrable, not random.

Julie Ward, a healer and spiritual teacher I know, once gave this illustration to describe to me what scientific prayer is like:

> When you bake your favorite cake, you follow the recipe, measuring out the cups and teaspoons for each ingredient accordingly. You have no doubt that, when you follow the instructions correctly, the cake you take out of the oven will be the same cake you've always made. You don't say to yourself, "I *hope* it will be a cake." You *know* it will be the same delicious dessert you've always made, because it is your tried-and-true recipe. Prayer works just like that. When you pray scientifically, you don't just *hope* God is listening; you *know* it. You *know* you'll find healing.[5]

This kind of prayer, done with an understanding of Principle, is reliable and dependable, an absolutely certain recognition that "God is our refuge and strength, a very present help in trouble" (Psalm 46:1). Prayer looked at as an affirmation of Truth — rather than as a kind of begging for help (to a remote Supreme Being who might or might not be there) — may seem unfamiliar, if we're used to viewing prayer as a last-ditch effort, reserved only for times when all other material avenues have been exhausted. We don't necessarily expect this type of prayer to work, but we do it anyway, just in case. This is *superstition,* not understanding! For scientific prayer to work, it is essential that we understand, rather than believe.[6]

Some of us may be accustomed to praying often, but much of it may be by rote, applying prayers and rituals learned from our parents' religion or from a cultural tradition. The words and ceremonies may have lost much of their original meaning. This kind of prayer is based on belief — and it is also hit and miss. To seek Truth through human doctrines is not very effective for gaining a full understanding of the Infinite. A spiritual understanding is better than any ritual or sacrament.[7]

If we acknowledge that there is only One Principle, we know that God isn't too busy to hear us and answer. God is ever-active and *always* paying attention. Remember, God isn't an anthropomorphic creature, nor is God somewhere *else*. God is within us and encircling us, communicating Love and Truth to us continuously and without ceasing! So all we have to do is tune in! It's just like radio waves — they are always being broadcast, but we can't hear anything unless we tune in the receiver to a particular frequency. With this scientific approach to prayer, we recognize that there isn't *another* acting principle called evil, able to vanquish God, or you or me, or anyone else. Right here, right now, Good is the *only* Power.

Since it is an impossibility for there to be something (or someplace) outside of Infinity, each of us is right where God is, and therefore we are equipped to know whatever it is we need to know. It's up to us to listen and ask for direction. Whether it's to slow down to avoid someone about to run a red light; to stop yelling and listen to what your teenager is telling you; to let go of the fear of catching a cold because your coworker just sneezed; to accept a job offer; or any number of other messages, significant or unadorned; prayer — in light of Principle — is a powerful force for Good in any situation. The more we pray with an understanding of Principle, the better life will be.

What Exactly is Prayer Again?

"That is real which never changes."
— Lao Tzu (6th c. BC)[8]

We've established that prayer is stopping to listen to Truth, to hear what God is telling us, along with an affirmation that help is already available.

It's striking to note that the same word is used for the action of praying as well as for the person doing it: *prayer* (supplication) and *pray-er* (the person). Here it's easy to acknowledge that God is One. We just can't be left out of the picture. Then the dictionary's definitions for prayer take on new meaning:

"request," "ask," "entreat," "implore," "beg," "beseech," "petition," "supplication," "a formal request directed to an authority," "an earnest call for help or support" — these all adhere to the conventional concept of prayer, and certainly remain useful. But what about: "ardent good wishes," "to address the Divine with adoration," "confession," and — best of all — "thanksgiving"? These ideas about prayer point us in a better direction.

Mary Baker Eddy describes prayer this way: "Thoughts unspoken are not unknown to the [D]ivine Mind. Desire is prayer; and no loss can occur from trusting God with our desires, that they may be moulded and exalted before they take form in words and in deeds."[9] She continues: "Prayer cannot change the Science of being, but it tends to bring us into harmony with it."[10] Of course we can't tell God anything. God already knows all, because God is Intelligence Itself. Because each individual is an expression of the One Mind, each of us, too, must already know everything that God knows.

This is the Absolute reality: *God is your mind.*

This profound realization is itself a humble and powerful prayer. In any time of need, great or small, it could go something like this:

> I thank You, God, for all the good that's happening. You truly are amazing and wonderful! Right now, though, I don't feel so good! Things don't seem to be going very well. It's time for me to turn back to You. That's why I'm turning away from all these failed attempts to fix this problem. I'm choosing now to realize that I need to reclaim my true identity as Your child. That is, I am asking for Your guidance, recognizing that I am already Your reflection — Your idea, Your creation. Therefore as a reflection of the Original One Mind, Love, Truth, Good, I can't express anything else. Because I acknowledge this is true, I know all the right ideas I need will be revealed to me. Teach me as I learn once again to accept Your perfect Love for me....

If you're sure you don't believe in the capricious or anthropomorphic God you may have grown up with, go easy on yourself. Instead, try Principle. This rock-solid basis can — and shall, if you are willing — lead you to your own sound understanding of God. An understanding that is based on real evidence, not on belief — something that makes sense for you, and *works* for you. You can prove it. In Divine Science, there's no such thing as failure. Can the Almighty be a failure? Of course not. Then you can't be, either. All it takes to see this is to switch to a spiritual viewpoint.[11] I love what inspirational speaker and author Wayne Dyer says about failure: "There's no such thing as failure.... The difference between a flower and a weed is only a judgment."[12]

The harmony and peace you seek aren't somewhere else, they're already here. Jesus said, "The kingdom of God doesn't come with observation, neither can you say 'Look here!' or 'Over there!' for, behold, the kingdom of God is within you" (see Luke 17:20–21). As spiritual teacher John Morton says, *Baruch Bashan* — the blessings already are.[13]

The undisturbed rhythm of the universe is already imprinted right here in our hearts. God is Love and Harmony — so God doesn't know, can't possibly know, *anything else*. Therefore there is no reason to fear or suffer.[14] There's nothing to be afraid of — we are safe and sound, we are free, we are OK, we are loved.

The bottom line is, we don't have to wander around in the mire of our lives, aimless or helpless, buffeted like the wind by chance or fate, never knowing what to do next. There is a universal Principle governing everything. During a difficult time, when we don't see God's control, we are accepting chaos instead of Principle, idiocy instead of Intelligence. All that we need to do is turn back to look in the Divine Mirror. Remember who you are: You are a perfect reflection of the One, which is All Good!

So pray scientifically. Be quiet and still.

There's no formula. But I can offer effective *guidelines* we can look to in order to organize our thoughts and calm down in any crisis, even in an emergency.

FIRST, DECLARE THE ABSOLUTE TRUTH.

Start with the solution, not the problem.

Principle is All. Principle is One. This One is All — and *here* and *now*. Be grateful for this fact! Even if you can't yet see it at this moment, *give thanks* for the Infinite Good you know is real. From time to time, you have been able to perceive this fact. So claim for Principle those "good times" even in this particular "bad time."[15]

Proclaim the Absolute Truth: The One Mind, Principle, Love, is in control — is true, is handling everything. Is holding you safe. All is well. You cannot be otherwise. You can't have fear once you accept this fact! So stay here until your thoughts stop racing, and you've calmed yourself enough to alleviate the fear.

SECOND, AFFIRM THE TRUTH AND DENY THE LIE.

Once fear is dismissed, you can acknowledge the fact of Principle to be true — *specifically* for your situation, for yourself, and for any others involved. Ask for inspiration and direction. Gather together in your thought as many ways you can think of where Principle and Intelligence can be confirmed here and now, even if the picture looks grim.

Be still. Keep listening for guidance. Don't give up. Refute, one by one, the false notion(s) that any evil(s) could overthrow God's all-power. Do this *specifically* for each problem or symptom, *replacing* each lie you throw out with a corresponding Truth.

Something you can start with when you're not sure what to do next is to consult dictionaries and thesauri for the meanings behind the problem. Then start listing the antonyms (opposites). Without exception, whenever I do this I am directed to the root of the error, and it's always so obvious — and then I can more easily refute it with an opposite Divine quality.

Let God speak to you personally through your study of the words. Then utilize synonyms for God (brainstorming lists are provided at the end of each chapter) in order to focus on specific qualities you know are true and want to see.

THIRD, CLAIM THE HEALING AS REAL AND PERMANENT.

Acknowledge God with gratitude for the healing of the situation, recognizing the final *authority* of Principle — It is the *unopposed* voice of Goodness! All other nay-saying opinions are put to rest in the face of this all-enveloping Power. Now and always, God is in control. You are comforted, safe, and free.

The example above is just a taste of what it means to pray scientifically. It all may happen in only a few seconds, or it may be a much longer process. There aren't any rules about form. You can pray with your eyes shut, or you can speak aloud — to yourself or to another. You can sing it, shout it, write it, or simply think it. Of course you can pray anytime, anywhere. You can pray while driving on the freeway, painting the den, doing the dishes, fixing the car, or mopping the floor. Just go for it!

Practice Divine Science. There's always more to explore. After all, we're talking about the Science of *Being* here. You can't expect to master it in one try, or understand it all in one day.[16] Dedication and practice are required. But even just a *glimpse* at the Science of Being shows us that there is an underlying Power that outshines all rituals, creeds, formulas, or prescribed prayers. The Principle of Love will guide you as an individual. You can't ever be separated from God, so even if you take a wrong turn, you can retrace your steps and get back on the right track.[17]

Think of reality as an infinite boundless ocean of consciousness. Picture a snowglobe, the kind you shake to watch the snowflakes swirl. Likewise, in this world all around you are thoughts, which hover and fall like snowflakes, flitting this way and that.[18] They are of human origin — all the thoughts of thousands upon thousands of years of history — opinions and stories that ebb and flow with the capricious tides of wind and time. Idle gossip, TV reruns, advertisements, political rhetoric, and a billion trillion other thoughts, good or bad, can drift in and out of the human mind. But you are not the victim of any axiom, no matter how time-honored. You can't be possessed by any assumptions whatsoever, because they have no hold on you. Since you know the difference between Truth and error, you can either grab on to each snowflake (thought), or let each one fall, powerless, by the wayside.

Like the proverbial little devil whining on your shoulder, mistaken thoughts can often be aggressive, but exposed to the light of Truth they'll melt like snowflakes hitting a flame. Accepted opinions fluctuate according to one's era and culture. On our planet in various locales, it's been common knowledge that we travel on the River Styx after death, that the Earth is the center of the universe, that women are chattel, that slavery is good for business, or even that life is simply a result of what DNA says it is. Who knows what else might be in store?

What else may come in the future is irrelevant. What matters is That Which Endures. That Which Endures is true — and *doesn't change*. Principle, Truth, is immovable. Principle, God, is without time. Cherish these ideas of God. All human opinions only swirl, confuse, and befuddle — they do not necessarily inform you of anything helpful. Let them all float away. Watch them go! They are no part of you! The snowstorm may create a dramatic picture, but it will spin around for a while and finally come to a stop. It has no bearing on Being Itself.

Credos After All

It goes without saying that you should always utilize prayers that are personally meaningful *to you,* and that you ought to continually rework them — express yourself spontaneously, sincerely, according to each situation. The point is, *make them your own.* After all, even though rituals and ceremonies are irrelevant in the larger scheme of things, a *personal* prayer — whether memorized from our religious upbringing, a 12-step program, a song, or a poem — can be immeasurably valuable when we're in turmoil. Your favorite prayers can be your five smooth stones. Why? Because what is familiar comes to us most easily in times of trouble. In an emergency, the words can flash automatically into our thought like lightning, reassuring us of what is still true. Then, in our openness, the Word becomes the instant calming influence we require in the midst of a storm.

Whatever form it takes, scientific prayer always starts at the top: We focus on the solution instead of on the problem.

Sometimes just remembering and applying *one line* of a treasured prayer, passage, or verse in thought can change everything. A woman I once met said she walked away from a head-on collision with a truck. She held firmly to the one phrase that came to her when she saw she couldn't avoid the accident: "God is Love." Her car was totaled but she was OK. A friend of mine who was a volunteer firefighter, in the midst of roaring flames, remembered the sentence from Eddy's book *Science and Health,* "Thus far and no farther."[19] The fire stopped at that point and did not destroy the rest of the building. A mother I know was concerned about a cold "going around" in her child's class. She realized that schoolmates cannot give colds to each other when this musical line came to mind: "I can't give you anything but love, baby..."; this insight prevented her child from catching a cold.

The following are some prayers I've found to be tried and true.[20] Many of the best prayers are Psalms written by our hero David, that underdog of a shepherd boy who killed Goliath and later became King of Israel. These prayers and others like it often provide a framework for me from which to begin whenever I find myself in a crisis, or overwhelmed in any way. Feel free to develop your own prayers from any of these. Of course, you can create your own versions of these prayers and others based on what means most to you and what you're working on, moment by moment.

The 23rd Psalm (a Psalm of David)

from the Bible (KJ):

The Lord is my shepherd; I shall not want.

He maketh me to lie down in green pastures:

He leadeth me beside the still waters.

He restoreth my soul:

he leadeth me in the paths of righteousness

for his name's sake.

Yea, though I walk through

the valley of the shadow of death,

I will fear no evil: for thou art with me;

thy rod and thy staff they comfort me.

Thou preparest a table before me

in the presence of mine enemies:

thou anointest my head with oil; my cup runneth over.

Surely goodness and mercy

shall follow me all the days of my life:

and I will dwell in the house of the Lord for ever.

interpretation by Mary Baker Eddy (19th-century healer and founder of the Christian Science Church in Boston, Massachusetts, USA — *brackets are hers*):

[Divine Love] is my shepherd;

I shall not want.

[Love] maketh me to lie down

in green pastures:

[Love] leadeth me

beside the still waters.

[Love] restoreth my soul [spiritual sense]:

[Love] leadeth me in the paths of righteousness

for His name's sake.

Yea, though I walk through the valley

of the shadow of death,

I will fear no evil:

for [Love] is with me;

[Love's] rod and [Love's] staff
they comfort me.
[Love] prepareth a table before me
in the presence of mine enemies:
[Love] anointeth my head with oil;
my cup runneth over.
Surely goodness and mercy shall follow me
all the days of my life;
and I will dwell in the house [the consciousness]
of [Love] for ever.[21]

from the Bible (the Contemporary English version [CEV]):

You, Lord, are my shepherd.
I will never be in need.
You let me rest in fields
of green grass.
You lead me to streams
of peaceful water,
and You refresh my life.

You are true to Your name,
and You lead me
along the right paths.
I may walk through valleys
as dark as death,
but I won't be afraid.
You are with me,
and Your shepherd's rod
makes me feel safe.

You treat me to a feast,
while my enemies watch.
You honor me as your guest,
and you fill my cup
until it overflows.

Your kindness and love
will always be with me
each day of my life,
and I will live forever
in Your house, Lord.

my version:

Love, You are my Shepherd;
I already have everything I need;
You calm me down,
forcing me to finally relax
in green pastures;
You lead me beside still waters;
You restore my hope
You lead me towards the right thing to do
for Love's sake.

Even if I go through dark times
clouded by the shadow of death,
I will not fear evil.
For You are with me.
Your rod and Your staff,
they comfort and guide me.

You prepare a table for me,
keeping me safe
even when I'm surrounded by enemies;
You give me inspiration.
Everything overflows with abundance!

Surely, goodness and mercy will be with me
all the days of my life.
And I will live in the arms of Love forever.

The Lord's Prayer — Matthew 6:9–13

(a Prayer of Jesus)

from the Bible (KJ):

> Our Father
> which art in heaven,
> Hallowed be thy name.
> Thy kingdom come.
> Thy will be done in earth,
> as it is in heaven.
> Give us this day our daily bread.
> And forgive us our debts,
> as we forgive our debtors.
> And lead us not into temptation,
> but deliver us from evil:
> For thine is the kingdom,
> and the power,
> and the glory, for ever. Amen.

interpretation by Mary Baker Eddy:

> Our Father-Mother God,
> all-harmonious,
> Adorable One.
> Thy kingdom is come;
> Thou art ever-present.
> Enable us to know,
> — as in heaven, so on earth, —
> God is omnipotent, supreme.
> Give us grace for to-day;
> feed the famished affections;
> And Love is reflected in love;
> And God leadeth us not into temptation,
> but delivereth us from sin, disease, and death.
> For God is infinite, all-power,
> all Life, Truth, Love, over all, and All.[22]

> Our Father-Mother God,
> You are Harmony
> Your Name is Holy
> Your rule is come
> Your will is done
> Here where we are, and everywhere.
> Give us today what we need,
> And forgive us our trespasses
> as we forgive those
> who trespass against us.
> You never lead us into temptation
> But deliver us from evil
> For Yours is all dominion,
> all power, and all glory,
> forever and ever. Amen.

Daily Prayer by Mary Baker Eddy

original version:

> "Thy kingdom come";
> let the reign of divine Truth, Life, and Love
> be established in me,
> and rule out of me all sin;
> and may Thy Word
> enrich the affections of all mankind,
> and govern them![23]

my version:

> Father-Mother God,
> Your will be done;
> Let the reign of Divine Truth, Life and Love
> Be established in me
> and rule out of me all sin;
> And may Your Word
> enrich the affections

of all people,
and govern us!

Psalm 51:10, 12 (a Psalm of David, after committing adultery)

Create in me a clean heart, O God,
and renew a right spirit within me.
Restore unto me the joy of Thy salvation
and uphold me with Thy free spirit.[24]

Psalm 19:14 (a Psalm of David, also sung in Jewish Renewal worship)

Let the words of my mouth
and the meditation of my heart
be acceptable in Thy sight, O God,
my strength, and my redeemer.

The Prayer of St. Francis of Assisi (12th-century Catholic friar and founder of the Franciscan order in Italy)

original version:

Lord,
Make me an instrument
of Thy peace,
Where there is hatred,
let me sow love;
Where there is injury, pardon;
Where there is doubt, faith;
Where there is despair, hope;
Where there is darkness, light;
Where there is sadness, joy;

O Divine Master,
Grant that I may not so much
seek to be consoled

as to console;
to be understood
as to understand;
to be loved as to love.

For it is in giving
that we receive;
it is in pardoning that we are pardoned;
and it is in dying that we are born to eternal life.[25]

my version:

Father-Mother God,
Make me an instrument
of Your peace.
Where there is hatred,
let me sow love;
Where there is injury, pardon;
Where there is doubt, faith;
Where there is despair, hope;
Where there is darkness, light;
Where there is sadness, joy.

Father-Mother God,
Let me not so much
seek to be consoled,
as to console;
to be understood
as to understand;
to be loved, as to love.

For it is in giving
that we receive;
it is in pardoning
that we are pardoned;

and it is in dying to the material unreality
that we are born to eternal life, wholly spiritual.

Children's Prayer by Mary Baker Eddy

original version:

    Father-Mother God,
    Loving me
    Guard me when I sleep;
    Guide my little feet
    Up to Thee.[26]

my version:

    Father-Mother God,
    Loving me
    Guard me when I sleep;
    [while I play, while at school,
    all day long, etc.]
    Guide my little feet
    Up to Thee.

Bed Time Prayer by Janis Hunt Johnson

    God is Love
    and you are loved
    and you are loving.
    God is Spirit
    and you are spiritual.
    God is Truth
    and you are truthful.
    God is Principle
    and you are principled.
    God is Soul
    and you are soulful!
    God is Life
    and you are fully alive,

and you are lively!
God is Mind
and you are God's good idea.
God is always with you,
keeping you safe —
every second of the day
and every second of the night.
Wherever you are, God is.
God is your Light
throughout the night.

The 5 Gs

God is Good.

God Guides, Guards, and Governs.[27]

The Scientific Statement of Being by Mary Baker Eddy

original version:

There is no life, truth, intelligence, nor substance in matter. All is infinite
Mind and its infinite manifestation, for God is All-in-all. Spirit is immortal
Truth; matter is mortal error. Spirit is the real and eternal; matter is the unreal
and temporal. Spirit is God, and man is His image and likeness. Therefore
man is not material; he is spiritual.[28]

my version:

There is no life, truth, intelligence, or substance in matter. All is infinite
Mind and Its infinite manifestation, for God is All-in-all. Spirit is forever
Truth; matter is a mistake, and presents a limited picture. Spirit is the real
and eternal; matter is the unreal and temporal. Spirit is God, and I am God's
image and likeness. Therefore I am not material; I am spiritual.

Before you call 911, recall Psalm 91:1!

from the Bible (KJ):

> He that dwelleth
> in the secret place
> of the most High
> shall abide
> under the shadow
> of the Almighty.

my version:

> When we know that we dwell
> in the secret place
> of the most high
> We abide
> safe in the shadow
> of the Almighty.

Psalm 139:23–24 (a Psalm of David)

from the Bible (KJ):

> Search me, O God,
> and know my heart:
> try me, and know my thoughts:
> And see if there be any wicked way in me,
> and lead me in the way everlasting.

Phil Keaggy's version:

> Search me, oh God, and know my heart,
> Try me and know my anxious thoughts,
> And see if there be any hurtful way in me.
> And lead me in the ever lasting way.[29]

Traditional Celtic Prayer

I weave a silence on my lips,
I weave a silence into my mind,
I weave a silence within my heart.
I close my ears to distractions,
I close my eyes to attentions,
I close my heart to temptations.
Calm me O Lord as You stilled the storm,
Still me O Lord, keep me from harm.
Let all the tumult within me cease,
Enfold me Lord in Your peace.

PRINCIPLE

fundamental	comprehensive
rule	doctrine
idea	axiom
law	noble
basis	foundation
virtuous	precept
convention	form
ethical	ground
righteous	moral
right-minded	character
elemental	usage
belief	acceptable
guiding sense	right conduct
method	originating force
actuating agency	quality
actual	constitution
substance	demonstration
plan	analogy
high-minded	thought
foothold	groundwork

substructure

essence

blueprint

SPIRIT

structure

formula

strategy

footing

origin

underlying

aspect

model

framework

design

nature

THESE BLANK PAGES FOR YOUR NOTES AND
PRAYERS

ENDNOTES

THE LAW OF PRINCIPLE
OBLITERATES AIMLESSNESS

1   See *S&H*, p. 476:6–10.

2   See *Commentaries on the Vedas, the Upanishads and the Bhagavad Gita: The Three Branches of India's Life-Tree,* by Sri Chinmoy. Jamaica, New York: Aum Publications, 1996, p. 245. Hereinafter referred to as *Commentaries on the Vedas.*

3   For a good summary of the major worldviews on mind and body, see the chart on p. 11 of Christian de Quincey's provocative article, "Consciousness: Truth or Wisdom?" in *IONS Noetic Sciences Review,* no. 51, March–June 2000, p. 8–13ff.

4   See *S&H*, p. 465:17–1. The use of the singular verb here is deliberate.

5   Although not an exact quote, this is how I recall Julie A. Ward's illuminating explanation.

6   See *S&H*, p. 285–286.

7   See *S&H*, p. 286:1–8. See also I Samuel 15:22, Hosea 6:6 and Mark 12:33.

8   Quoted by Wayne W. Dyer on the PBS broadcast, Feb. 11, 2001 (Medford, Oregon), "Improve Your Life Using the Wisdom of the Ages," in which he discusses his book, *The Wisdom of the Ages: 60 Days to Enlightenment.* New York: HarperCollins, 1998. Hereinafter referred to as "Improve Your Life."

9   *S&H*, p. 1:10–14.

10 *S&H*, p. 2:15–16. For a seminal discussion, read *S&H*, chapter 1, entitled "Prayer."

11 For an inspirational book on switching to a spiritual perspective, read *Living in Grace: The Shift to Spiritual Perception — A Guide to Personal Practical Spirituality,* by Beca Lewis. Encinitas, CA: Perception Publishing, 2002.

12 "Improve Your Life."

13 This saying in Hebrew is thoroughly explored in *The Blessings Already*

Are, by John Morton. Los Angeles: Mandeville Press, 2000.

14   See *Retrospection and Introspection,* by Mary Baker Eddy. Boston: The First Church of Christ, Scientist, 1891, 1892, p. 61–62. Hereinafter referred to as *Retrospection and Introspection.*

15   When Jesus raised Lazarus from the dead, he started out matter-of-factly by praying, "Father, I know you've always heard me...." Jesus didn't panic one bit over the fact that Lazarus had been dead for four days. The truth was clear to him, and thus Lazarus came forth alive (see John 11:1–44, namely verses 41–44).

16   See *Unity of Good,* by Mary Baker Eddy. Boston: The Christian Science Publishing Society, 1887, p. 3:20–5:18, especially 5:9–13. Hereinafter referred to as *Unity of Good.*

17   See *Miscellaneous Writings,* p. 10:12–16.

18   See *S&H,* p. 250:29–30.

19   The full passage from *S&H,* p. 124:20, reads: "Adhesion, cohesion, and attraction are properties of Mind. They belong to divine Principle, and support the equipoise of that thought-force, which launched the earth in its orbit and said to the proud wave, 'Thus far and no farther.'"

20   Sources for prayers are endless. One you might want to start with is *The Bridge of Stars: 365 Prayers, Blessings and Meditations from Around the World,* ed. by Marcus Braybrooke. London: Duncan Baird Publishers, 2001.

21   *S&H,* p. 578:4–18.

22   See *S&H,* p. 16:26–15.

23   *The Manual of the Mother Church,* by Mary Baker Eddy. Boston: The Christian Science Publishing Society, 1895, p. 42:19–25.

24   Psalm 51:10–12 has a musical version in three different settings, which I often sang growing up as part of the liturgy in the Lutheran church. See *The Lutheran Book of Worship* Ed. by Philip H. Pfatteicher and Carlos R. Messerli. Minneapolis: Augsburg Publishing House / Philadelphia: Board of Publication, Lutheran Church in America, 1978, p. 75, 96, and 118. This Psalm is also sung in Jewish Renewal worship with a different tune.

25   From *There's a Spiritual Solution to Every Problem* by Wayne W. Dyer. New York: HarperCollins Publishers, 2001, p. 139.

26   From *Miscellaneous Writings,* p. 400:12–18, this verse, actually titled "Mother's New Year Gift to the Little Children," also has been set to music, and can be heard on a wonderful audiotape for young children entitled

Before We Read: Prayers and Hymns by Mary Baker Eddy (published in Boston, MA by The First Church of Christ, Scientist, The Christian Science Board of Directors, ©1980), which also includes a song version of Eddy's Prayer "to the Big Children," from *Miscellaneous Writings*, p. 400:20–25.

27   See *The House with the Colored Windows*. Boston: The Christian Science Publishing Society, 1953, p. 11–13.

28   *S&H*, p. 468:9–15.

29   Words excerpted from the song "Psalm 139" by Phil Keaggy, from his CD album *Backroom Trax 5*.

2

Keystone:

the piece at the crown of an arch
that locks the other pieces in place;
something on which associated things
depend for support, binding the whole.

SPIRIT

Let's be sensible.

"Those who look
through matter into Spirit
really know
the mystery of the unreal
and the Real."
— Paramahansa Yogananda, 1893–1952[1]

THE LAW OF SPIRIT
ANNIHILATES MATERIALITY

The Realm Of The Real

God is Spirit. Therefore Spirit is our very essence, the core of what is real about us and what keeps each of us going, moment by moment. So it's no surprise that the word *spirit* comes from the Latin, *spirare,* "to breathe." This is also the origin for the word *inspiration.* In Hebrew, *ruach* means "breath," "spirit," and "wind." In Greek, the word is *pneuma,* meaning "breath," as well as "mind" and "vital principle."

The realm of the real is Spirit.[2] There's *only one* creation and it is spiritual, not material. It's not the crazy mixed-up world we call planet Earth, which seems perpetually full of chaos and misery. It's infinite, multifaceted Good, eternally unfolding Love, power, wisdom, invention, innovation, wonderment, beauty, ecstasy, and bliss — pure and perfect harmony. This is God being God, the Is "is-ing," the One Mind thinking. And God *can't be,* without each of us. Since we are Mind's ideas, we are always, inseparably, a part of The Plan, The Love, The Principle, the Harmony and Heaven, which continue forward, expanding forever. Spirit pervades all space, and needs no material method (such as ether, wires, electricity, etc.) for the transmission of messages in order to be omnipresent.[3] Spirit, Mind, is genuinely everywhere at once in space and time; It has no need to go or to be sent. To the degree that we are aware of this spiritual reality, we can see that we live in a completely spiritual creation.

The Falsehood Of Original Sin

"I just found out there's no such thing as the real world /
Just a lie you got to rise above." — John Mayer[4]

The story of Adam and Eve was a fable written by men and later purported as literal fact by institutionalized Christianity, in order to condemn us all as sinners who require redemption. The lie of Original Sin is probably *the most* insidious obstacle to our spiritual understanding and well-being.

Why? Because if we really are sinners, and God made us that way, what's the point of trying to be anything better? What good does it do even to worry about our flaws? If *God* made them, then they must be OK, and God put us into a mess on purpose, just for sport. There's also even the notion here that God is a failure, which would preclude God's omnipotence.[5]

If God is anthropomorphic, and so primitive as to require blood sacrifices for sins' remission — either through Jewish rituals (as in the Old Testament) or through Jesus' blood on the cross (as in the New Testament) — then any reasonable person ought to chuck the whole lot. It's time to cast off old folktales that make no sense. Superstition and blind faith have no place in modern society; we have outgrown them.

If we accept the validity of Original Sin, then it follows from this premise that God created us first of all wired for failure, and not only that, God created Evil — Satan — an arch enemy, simply to hang around for the purpose of constantly battling against all the forces of Goodness. But this is illogical. Why would the All, the Whole of Being — Love, Life and Truth Itself — bother with hate, death, and falsehood? What would be the point? And how could it be possible? Love can't be *all*-encompassing if it harbors even *one* element of hatred. Then Love wouldn't be Love. And God wouldn't be God.

God can't be God, can't even exist, period, unless we let God be what God is supposed to be, by definition: all-Good, Supreme, Omnipresence, Omnipotence, Omniscience. Omnipresent Good — everlasting, and thus filling all space infinitely — doesn't leave *any room* for even *one bit* of evil. *You can't have more than all!*[6] Thus Omnipotent Good is *unopposed.*

Omniscience, encompassing the ultimate Intelligence of the universe, already knowing these obvious facts, would know from the start that evil simply can't be: Evil is an impossibility, without legitimacy, without relevance — and certainly no attention need be paid to any claim that evil is present.

Remember, I'm not saying that we should ignore the evil we see around us. Evil, although in reality an impotent illusion, *is* powerful — whenever we *give* it power. And its power grows if it is not dealt with squarely. We gloss over evil to our own peril. Evil must be uncovered and purged for the lie that it is, or it will flourish. We can't fully understand evil's unreality until we repent and forsake it.[7]

Something Funny Happens On The Way To Free Will

> "We are properly self-governed only when guided rightly and governed by our Maker, divine Truth and Love.... Reflecting God's government, we are self-governed." — Mary Baker Eddy[8]

I once overheard someone say that God *created* evil, so that we could have free will; otherwise, "we'd all be robots, just bowing down to God like slaves." When someone commits an act of murder or other heinous crime, I've heard it said more than once, "that's the price we pay for having free will."

These assumptions are based on the idea that God is somehow a *mixture* of good and evil, a capricious supreme being who created us either out of boredom or from a need for reassurance. But God doesn't require entertainment or worship. God isn't a Puppeteer, manipulating our strings.

God doesn't have time for the *non*sense of our disobedience. It isn't an issue, because it doesn't even come up. The truth of the matter is, we are *incapable* of acting against God. We actually don't have the "freedom" to go astray or choose wrongly, because we are *not separate* from the Divine.[9]

The Deity (Spirit) can't be limited to one tiny planet Earth. Spirit is forever pouring forth at every point in the universe simultaneously, like eternal sunlight that shines in every direction indiscriminately. And each of us, like an individual ray of sunshine, beams just as brightly and derives all our power from just that One point of origin.[10] Just as the sun's rays are inseparable from the light source — yet every sunbeam is a part of the fullness of its illumination — so we are each a unique and necessary emanation of Spirit.

What does *universe* mean? The word *universe* comes from Latin, meaning "one turning" (*unus versum*), "turned into one," or "combined into one whole." I'm not saying a *material* universe is God. On the contrary — I'm saying the universe is a reflection of Intelligence Itself, Being Itself, Spirit Itself. The universe radiates from Being — The One I AM simply Being Itself and Knowing Itself.

Each of us is a good idea; we can't help it. Each of us has the Divine Mind, the Great Spirit, as our Source — and therefore the entire universe is at our doorstep. In that sense we might assume we have "free will," but what we actually *have* is the Divine Will — for free! — so we're set free, and freely given endless opportunities to experience and share good. In Spirit, each of us embodies unlimited Freedom Itself — an ever-expanding, ever-unfolding Intelligence, always flowing forth with new ideas, innovations and discoveries — imparting only goodness. No one can fall away from this reign of Love. That's a lot better than the common view that we have the "free will" to wander away from God and get into trouble.

Let's go back to the Mirror analogy (see *Reflection* in the introductory chapter on Mind): When you stand in front of several mirrors at a department store, your image is shown on each glass simultaneously, each one mimicking exactly what you do. One of the images of you can't decide on its own to go off and do something else; all the mirror images are bound to do exactly the same thing you do.[11] Like an infinity of mirrors, each of us reflects God, with no separation between the Original and the image. We as individuals made in the "image and likeness" of God (as mentioned in Genesis 1:27), then, are sinless. Because we are actual expressions of the unflawed and crystal-clear image of God, rather than mortals, we are unshackled from any limitations of materiality — each of us is at liberty every moment to be a brand new Divine idea. And when we know this freedom for ourselves, we "see what God sees" — only the spiritual reality — and this understanding transforms any human situation. When we realize we can give up false self-will and replace it with God's will, this is true freedom.

Disgruntled Christians and Jews, take heart. Let's look at the creation story in the Bible *from a spiritual perspective*. The book of Genesis starts out: "In the beginning God created the heaven and the earth" (1:1). God's reality is seen in God's acts; Deity is not an entity that can be conceived of apart from Divine works.[12] The word *beginning* means "origin" or "source," not necessarily relating to a particular point in time. The Old English word for beginning, *ginnan,* is thought to have come from the word for yawn, *ginan,* implying "an opening," or "an open and deep space." Perhaps more than any other, this one Bible verse sums it up. The Source of All simply *is*. The *origin* of All (Latin, *origin,* from *oriri,* "to rise") is an *opening* to Truth.

Twenty-six short verses later, Genesis says that God created us "male and female" in God's "own image" (1:27). By the end of this first chapter of the Bible, six "days" have passed, and God has already created everything, "and behold, it was very good" (1:31). God rests and blesses the seventh day.

Then all of a sudden, "a mist" rises up from the earth, and God starts forming a man "of the dust of the ground" (2:6–7). Wait a minute! According to the first chapter, God's work was already finished — God *already* created us "male and female"! So what's this contradictory story doing here? This subsequent second version of creation — the Adam-and-Eve myth in Genesis chapters 2 and 3 — has been ingrained into our Western culture long enough. It is time to toss it out for the travesty that it is.

Let's take a fresh look at it — as an allegory about the perils of accepting a material perspective as real. The Adam-and-Eve story of sin and loss tells of the confusion and suffering that result when we think there is somehow a power other than God (a talking serpent), or when we think we are separate from God (thrown out of the Garden of Eden). The accursed Adam-and-Eve picture is the *opposite* of the truth about our lot. The truth of our destiny as *wholly good* has already been stated completely in Genesis Chapter 1. In *Science and Health,* Mary Baker Eddy observes:

> It may be worth while here to remark that, according to the best scholars, there are clear evidences of two distinct documents in the early part of the book of Genesis. One is called the Elohistic, because the Supreme Being is therein called Elohim. The other document is called the Jehovistic, because Deity therein is always called Jehovah — or Lord God, as our common version translates it [*Jehovah* is actually a bastardization of the unpronounceable Hebrew word for God, *YHWH*]. Throughout the first chapter of Genesis and in three verses of the second — in what we understand to be the spiritually scientific account of creation — it is Elohim (God) who creates. From the fourth verse of chapter two to chapter five, the creator is called Jehovah, or the Lord. The different accounts become more and more closely intertwined to the end of chapter twelve, after which the distinction is not definitely traceable.[13]

Let's resolve here and now to discard Original Sin and replace it with our true identity: Original Good.

The word *original* not only comes from *origin* ("source" or "beginning"), it can also mean "created," and "capable of thinking or acting in an independent, creative, or individual manner." Each of us is a unique individual. Only you can understand and express Divinity in your own particular way. Just think: God wouldn't be complete without you!

The word *sin* means "transgression of the law of God" or "a vitiated state of human nature in which the self is estranged from God." The Greek word for sin is *hamartano,* meaning "to miss the mark" and in Hebrew it is *châtâ,* "to miss" and "to lead astray." These shades of meaning are actually reassuring, when we know that in reality it's impossible to sin, impossible *to* break the laws of God. Once we understand that we don't have to listen to the serpent's nagging little voice of doubt and deceit, we can see that sin is not our true nature; we can cast it off much more quickly.

When we see things as they really are — in the spiritually scientific sense — we can't blame the serpent (as Eve did) for a lapse in judgment, nor can we blame another person (as Adam blamed Eve) for our failings. If you've gone astray down a wrong path, it takes only a change of heart — a change in your *thinking* — to turn back to Spirit, and see that you never really left. There's no effort required on your part, except to yield to this Truth. The efforts we do make are the often great lengths we take to *ignore* God, the noise we make in our own thoughts and actions to drown out the Divine message being continuously broadcast throughout the universe: "All is well."

It is when we put aside all self-condemnation, and any judgment or blame of others, when we humbly look to the One Spirit, that our alignment with the One Principle is clear. Then we are free.

In today's emerging paradigm, the model for the universe is One Mind thinking. Mind is always generating ideas. Since Mind can't be separated from Its ideas, we are blissfully safe, comforted, and protected in all circumstances — and never "missing" some arbitrary "mark" set by religious doctrines or outgrown traditions. As Eddy writes, we can't be aimless, wandering, cast out of Eden; we are perpetually aligned to Spirit, always obeying Its Law:

> Through discernment of the spiritual opposite of materiality, even the way through [the] Christ, Truth, man will reopen with the key of [D]ivine Science the gates of Paradise which human beliefs have closed, and will find himself unfallen, upright, pure, and free, not needing to consult almanacs for the probabilities either of his life or of the weather, not needing to study brainology to learn how much of a man he is.[14]

Atonement — Our Divine Childhood

If Mind, Principle, Spirit is One, ever expressing Itself *through* each of us, we can claim this identity as a parent-child relationship. God — although not human — can nevertheless be viewed as our Father-Mother, expressing the permanent parental *qualities* of guardianship, protection, shelter, nourishment, guidance, and unconditional love. We can count on this One Parent, our Source, more than anyone else, to be right here for us, every moment.

Forever free from Original Sin, we can embrace this Father-Mother, our Original Good, the Divinity which never abandons us, never fails us, never disillusions us. Even in our darkest hour, each of us can reach out to this ever-presence of Love. We need only look as far as our own hearts to intuit that this is true. This purity is the Truth of our being. No matter what we've been through or what we've done, when we turn to Our Source for guidance, the answers will come. This is repentance.

Repentance not only means "to be sorry" or to make amends for wrongdoing. The Greek word for *repent, metanoeite,* means "to change one's mind" — in other words, to *re*pent is "to think again."[15] The opposite of repentance is actually complacency and self-satisfaction.[16] When we don't repent, we are content to stay in the illusory world of sin. Repentance demands a sincere determination to change one's mind and behavior. *Teshuvah*, a Hebrew word for repentance, literally means "return," and describes an experience that's meant to bring about a return to one's true self. When we do choose to repent, in our newly humbled thought the Light of Truth can once again shine on every seemingly impossible-to-solve situation. Repentance brings us back home — out of the darkness of sin, into the arms of Love.

This is the Law of Spirit. At all times, in all places, as children of Spirit we must claim our right to be free from all sin. This is our birthright — what I call *our divine childhood*.[17]

We can take positive action the instant we realize our true heritage: We can declare "I can" and "I will" because each of us is the child of I AM. Genuine *practical* repentance, says Mary Baker Eddy, reforms the heart and enables us to do the will of wisdom.[18] Thus I see atonement as a daily process of reconciliation and renewal.

Atonement for sin, i.e., "reconciliation with God," is not accomplished simply by one Day of Atonement (the Jews' Yom Kippur), by fasting during one particular month (the Muslims' Ramadan), nor by participating in the Christians' sacrament of Holy Communion. Of course, we can certainly find such rituals helpful in getting us closer to God. But the real key to practical repentance and atonement is that *moment by moment,* we want to focus on letting go of the false self (the belief that there *is* a material self) in order to embrace the One Self. This at-one-ment with God gives us the strength to ask for forgiveness and to forgive others. Originally the word *atonement* was *not* a religious term coined to identify us as sinners constantly in need of redemption. Surprisingly, according to the dictionary, *atonement* literally does mean "at-one-ment" — that is, the quality of being "at one," "at unity," and "in harmony." Eddy puts it this way: "Atonement is the exemplification of man's unity with God."[19]

What Is The Body?

Our bodies are not materially physical. We are spiritually mental. That doesn't mean you're going to float away into oblivion if you realize this fact. Remember, ideas are just as tangible to other ideas as matter claims to be to material things. You can still hug, feel warmth, etc. But we need to understand that everything is spiritually mental and not made out of stuff that breaks, cuts, dies, and rots. Thus the spiritual is "that which doesn't come and go"; the spiritual is "that which lasts."[20] When we grasp this concept about ourselves, the possibilities for healing and renewal are limitless.

Your thought is what your body demonstrates: Your body is your present understanding of what is spiritually true. As the title of the book by Deb Shapiro declares, *your body speaks your mind.* But you are not its victim. Your body adjusts as your understanding adjusts.

We are not subject to so-called physical laws; they are transitory and arbitrary; they change as cultures and "scientific facts" change. Our loyalties lie instead with the Law of Spirit: We are governed only by this unchanging Law.

Even when we view our body as physical, we find out that it is constantly renewing itself. According to biologists, 98% of all the molecules that make up the body replace themselves about once a year — with some aspects (such as the liver and the skeleton) completely new every few months. Our skin replaces itself entirely once a month; we have a new stomach lining every five days.[21] So how is it that we continue to look like ourselves, continue to maintain an identity, and often, continue to have the same physical problems? Why do we continue to reconstruct ourselves in old ways? Isn't it simply because of belief, education, and conditioning?[22] It is estimated that the average person thinks about 60,000 thoughts each day; 95% of the thoughts we have today are the same ones we had yesterday. According to Dr. Deepak Chopra, this is why we keep "creating the same patterns that give rise to the same physical expression of the body."[23]

From conception to death, we are believed to be ruled by physical criteria, thought and taught to do so and to be so; heretofore our common thinking has not allowed for any other possibility. But new discoveries in the fields of quantum physics and consciousness are declaring an untapped reality whose power we are only just beginning to comprehend.

Although it is presumed to be matter, the body consists instead of beliefs; it is made up of the highest stratum of matter; that is, the body is a manifestation of the objective state of the so-called human mind.[24] If we choose to view the body as physical, this is a very limited way of looking at things, and we are indeed doomed to suffer and die. But if we accept the body as spiritual, a whole new potential for transformation emerges.

Shall we define ourselves by our heredity, our experiences, our past, our circumstances? How about a resounding *no*? We can start practicing right now — with the tools of Divine Science — to see our true spiritual nature. Any time we choose, we can renovate our thinking! In this "house" of consciousness we call the "body," we can remodel the constructs of thought, and bring about any change necessary to improve our own well-being. Instead of allowing the body to renew itself in old ways, perpetually stuck in the past, let's toss the baggage, and throw off outmoded ways of thinking.[25] As we let go of it, the heaviness of this burden is gone; we feel *lighter*. We've made new room for Spirit's *Light*, shining forth to show us the way. This is the beginning of en*lighten*ment![26]

So let's define ourselves instead by Spirit, which remains steadfast, and which cannot ever come to an end. As Eddy says: "God expresses in man the infinite idea forever developing itself, broadening and rising higher and higher from a boundless basis."[27] Instead of being programmed by matter for suffering, decline, and death, we are actualized by Spirit — created only for joy, advancement, and Life everlasting.

By accepting Spirit's reality, you aren't rejecting your body. You don't have to *give up* anything; you're *gaining* a whole new perspective, which you can claim with confidence and reverence. So the spiritual reality is all the more "solid" because you know it is genuine, not temporary. So revel in this grand fact. Embrace the body for what it really is — Spirit's expression — and things will change.

The following account from my own experience years ago illustrates this point:

> One splendid spring afternoon, I took my twenty-month-old daughter to a three-year-old neighbor boy's birthday party. There were lots of kids there from about age two to seven. It was held in his yard, with toys, trucks, swings, etc. I was happy to be away from work, and enjoyed relaxing outside. But after a while, as I sat listening to the mothers discuss the various allergies, sicknesses, and past injuries of their children, I started looking at everybody, and began thinking that it was just too stressful. Each of us has to be so careful to look out for our child — to make sure he or she doesn't wander off, hit some other kid, fall, etc. All at once it looked like such a precarious juggling act! I was soon feeling just as worried as the other mothers.
>
> When I realized what I was doing, I corrected my thinking right away. I turned my thoughts full circle, and decided to see the same exact scene as a ballet, a dance orchestrated and protected by Love, and by each of us through our mindfulness for our children. My spirits quickly lifted, and I continued to watch out for everyone, back to enjoying the sunshine.
>
> I was watching a bigger boy swing back and forth as hard as he could on the swingset's teeter-totter, without a child on the other side. He was joyfully and proudly pushing as hard and as high as he could go. All of a sudden my daughter walked

obliviously right into it, as he swung — full force — right into her cheek. One of the mothers screamed. I picked my daughter up right away and held her, telling her she was all right. Then we went inside to avoid a scene.

She soon stopped crying, but there was a big red spot on her cheek, and she was still upset. I wiped her tears and told her she was pure and perfect, and that our Father-Mother God was holding her safe and comfortable, like a big blanket, loving her right then. We have always prayed together like this, so I know she recognized the gist of what I was saying. Her eyes brightened and she calmed down.

A few minutes later we went back outside, and the injury was forgotten. No one even mentioned it, because my daughter was composed and happy again, looking sweet in her new party dress.

Later at home that evening there was only a slight red mark on her cheek. The next day there wasn't even a bruise — no sign of the injury!

As I look back on it, had this injury happened just a few minutes earlier, I know I would have been panicked beyond description, probably rushed for ice, the emergency room, who knows. But because I had just switched gears in my thinking, I actually had almost no fear when this happened. I'm so thankful for this sure sign of God's care for us!

Only Wholeness

"We are all sculptors, working at various forms, moulding and chiseling thought. What is the model before mortal mind? Is it imperfection, joy, sorrow, sin, suffering? Have you accepted the mortal model? Are you reproducing it? Then you are haunted in your work by vicious sculptors and hideous forms. Do you not hear from all mankind of the imperfect model? The world is holding it before your gaze continually. The result is that you are liable to follow those lower patterns, limit your life-work, and adopt into your experience the angular outline and deformity of matter models. To remedy this, we must first turn our gaze in the right direction, and then walk that way. We must form perfect models in thought and look at them continually, or we shall never carve them out in grand and noble lives." — Mary Baker Eddy[28]

To prevent or cure disease, we have to allow Spirit's power to break the spell of the material senses.[29] Instead of using medicine to cure a physical body — applying matter to fix something supposedly material — we need to utilize prayer to fix our thinking. Only then can true health emerge. This type of healing is permanent. Instead of applying Band-Aids to treat symptoms which can recur, scientific prayer applies the Truth, extracting the error at the root. When mistaken thinking is eliminated, we can see the Truth clearly. "You don't have to brainwash yourself about this," explains Dr. Chopra. "You just have to have the insight." *The insight itself* can cause spontaneous adjustments in the body to restore health.[30]

Thus with mind-body medicine — a holistic approach to health care — and all sorts of alternative treatments on the rise, even conventional wisdom is now spotting chinks in its materialistic armor. Dr. Candace Pert, a professor and neurobiologist who specializes in brain biochemistry, has pointed out that the traditional idea that mind and body are separate no longer applies, since her experiments have shown that the same types of cells that manufacture and receive emotional chemistry in the brain are actually present throughout our entire body. In other words, the body's immune system has the capacity to learn.[31] So do the heart, stomach, kidneys, intestines, etc. Thus the same neurotransmitters that work in the brain are also active in many other locations in the human body.[32] "When you say 'I have a gut feeling about such and such,'" explains Chopra, "you're not speaking metaphorically; you're speaking literally because your gut makes the same chemicals that your brain makes when it thinks. In fact, your gut feeling may be a little more accurate because the gut cells haven't yet evolved to the stage of self-doubt."[33]

Once we know the fact that we are spiritual, we can't *un*know it. Then we can understand why it's not in our nature to suffer from any disease or injury. The notion becomes absurd. Once our eyes are opened, we can see that all along there remains only health.

Swiss psychologist Carl Jung (1875–1961), a pioneer in modern psychology and prolific writer, discusses in his book *Modern Man in Search of a Soul* the healing process as he observed it in his patients: Jung found that in the end, every difficulty, whatever it may be, is "resolved irrationally." With patience, he says, we bear the darkness "until the light appears" and "the solution is *given*." Jung describes this process as our "instinctual drive towards wholeness."[34]

The words *healing* and *health* both come from the Old English, *hal*, meaning "whole." When we are healthy, we are recognizing our innate wholeness — we are intact, unhurt, free of defect or impairment, complete, perfect. When we realize that Spirit is the only power, this turns the lightbulb on in our thinking that brings the healing to the situation. Know that you don't have to suffer, and you won't. It sounds too simple. But it *is* just that simple.

Now let's look at a religious model. The usual concept declared by mainline Christianity is that Jesus was actually God in human form, who came to earth to die on a cross in order to forgive sin. (A rather barbaric notion when you think about it; why should a blood sacrifice do the trick?) But in our en*lightenm*ent, let's consider the following instead: Jesus was an enlightened individual who died and rose again *in order to show us that death isn't real.*

The reason Jesus could heal people was because he saw their spiritual wholeness; this cutting-edge rabbi wasn't performing miracles in defiance of nature but actually demonstrating the natural Law of Spirit.[35] Finally, his resurrection proclaimed once and for all: We are whole. Jesus' early followers experienced this first-hand. Theologian Morton Kelsey, in *Healing and Christianity,* points out: "they realized that the realm of the Spirit ruled over all reality and that in the end there was nothing to fear."[36] Kelsey goes on to discuss Jesus' resurrection, subsequent appearance, his ability to walk through walls, and the ascension, in light of modern physics: "Those who know anything of the 'emptiness' and energic quality of matter will certainly not dismiss it as implausible."[37] And if scientists can manipulate atoms and collect them together in just the right sequence to create the bomb, let alone accomplish cloning, etc., such phenomena as resurrection, or instantaneous healing, suddenly don't seem so far-fetched.[38]

The existence of God doesn't have to be mere speculation any more, but simply *the Name* (in Hebrew, *Hashem*) which religious people have applied to their experience when recognizing a healing reality that is beyond present human consciousness. Even the eminent German physicist Werner Heisenberg (1901–1976) felt that the assumption that a spiritual world exists can "express a more direct connection with reality than even the most precise abstractions of science."[39]

Religion and science often seem far apart. That's because individuals in both fields can find themselves stalled in the quagmire of narrow assumptions and models. But there is also earnest inquiry from seekers on both sides. The progress will continue. Let's elevate and expand our thinking — and we can uncover the synthesis between spirituality and science.

One Cause And Effect

"Spiritual ideas, like numbers and notes, start from Principle,
and admit no materialistic beliefs." — Mary Baker Eddy[40]

Spirit is All, and thus unopposed. Charles Birch, winner of the Templeton Prize for Progress in Religion in 1990, says "God is both cause in creating the world and effect in experiencing the world."[41] Eddy states that since there is only One Cause, there can be no effect from any *other* cause, no reality in anything which doesn't proceed from the One Cause.[42] If Spirit is both Cause and Effect, how can knowledge of this fact make a difference in our everyday life?

Here's one simple example, which keeps me from catching a cold or flu, and prevents disease. The common belief is that there are germs everywhere — bacteria, viruses, diseases. And most of these microscopic critters even have names. Through education and socialization, we're taught that these invisible forces can attack at any time without warning to *cause* suffering — and all we can do when this happens is either ride it out (as with a cold or flu), or combat these scoundrels with medicines, antibiotics, or other material treatments. In this scenario, we are physical beings which can be attacked by other physical (albeit microscopic) beings, which seem to have minds of their own. If we stick with this premise, we will always be victims. God is somewhere else, or even nonexistent, and prayer is futile — a child's game designed to make us feel better while we suffer through our condition, and hope against hope that it passes. If it doesn't, then *we* pass away. That's just how life goes, we say.

But now let's start from the opposite premise: The realm of the real is Spirit; so Spirit is the *only* cause, substance, and consciousness, and matter is a mistaken human concept.[43] Now germs or diseases can be seen for what they truly are. If they're made of the same stuff we are — consciousness — then all we have to do is correct our thought to dismiss them. As soon as I know that my body and anything that comes in contact with it aren't subject to material laws, then a germ or virus has no more power over me. If I'm subject only to the Law of Spirit, I am not susceptible to invasion of any sort. I am free. *The only Cause is Good.* Therefore the mere assumption that something is attacking me cannot *cause* anything *else* to happen. The mistaken supposition (that there is *another* cause other than All Good) is harmless in the realm of Spirit, because it must obey the Law of Spirit. Spirit's Law says: All inharmony (including disease) is unreal, powerless. When I reject the belief that I can catch an ailment involuntarily, I survive "cold and flu season" unscathed. When something is said to be "going around," you don't have to catch it; throw away the catcher's mitt and let that ball fly right by!

The word *disease* itself tells us exactly what we're dealing with here. From the Latin, it literally means "dis-ease," that is, "lack of ease," "discomfort," "trouble," or "uneasiness." Webster's dictionary also mentions "derangement or disorder of the mind." This is the key precisely. The human mind (a fabrication that comes from an erroneous premise) is changeable, impressionable. So whenever disease threatens to strike, pray. Be quiet. Get yourself out of the situation — that is, your false self of blood, guts, brain, and intellect that thinks it is somehow separate, lost, confused, vulnerable, hurting — and yield to the One Self, the One Mind, where you already know that all is well.

Starting from Spirit, the One Cause, we can see that any symptoms of a virus, a disease, an allergy-causing substance, etc., are all the *results* of mistaken thinking; they're *not causes* of suffering in and of themselves. What a relief! Then the healing can happen. It can even be instantaneous. We see the sheer ridiculousness of assigning to a microscopic force — or to a flower, weed, or pet's dander — a power greater than All. Our thinking is transformed. The problem disintegrates.

Align your thinking to the One Mind. Prayer can be that simple. Using this method, I have been healed in a few hours or even in minutes of: colds, flu, migraines, stomach upset, heartburn, toothache, injury, etc. — without medicine or other material remedy. The many ailments and problems that are *prevented* this way through scientific prayer are innumerable.

I am convinced that it is not extravagant to predict that within this century, in everyday conversation when someone brings up the subject of germs or viruses causing disease, another person will be able to say without embarrassment, "Oh, I don't really believe in that stuff any more," and no one will bat an eye. One day, attributing any power to germs and diseases will be viewed with as much skepticism as staking one's life on signs of the zodiac and astrological charts. I'm not saying that medical and astrological approaches aren't helpful to people in the common way of looking at things. But once we gain a spiritual understanding of existence and adopt a higher spiritual view, our experience is elevated beyond the material picture, and scientific prayer becomes the most effective and immediate remedy.

When you look at life from Spirit's perspective, can DNA have any bearing on your experience? Genetic discoveries and the like may be interesting or beneficial, but that doesn't mean that we must accept DNA as the last word on who we are. As God's children, we are not constituents of matter (of the insubstantial, of the unsubstantiated), but citizens of Spirit (of Substance). As God's children we can inherit only good from the one Father-Mother-Source. Because we are governed according to the sovereignty of Spirit, a DNA indictment — claiming to give us specific proclivities and dispositions, predicting with certainty that particular characteristics, diseases, or aberrations will develop because of hardwired physical heredity — is thrown out of Spirit's court for lack of evidence. Once we accept this fact, we are not just out on bail, we are exonerated of all charges![44]

Here are some ideas I shared some years ago with a dear friend of mine in a letter regarding my prayers for her young son who was diagnosed with severe learning disabilities, including impaired speech development due to a brain defect:

> *Speech* and *talk* are forms of *communication,* a word which literally means "to share in common," "an interchange of thoughts," "intelligence," and "a connecting passage." Let's decide to see these ideas as part of [your son's] nature, his natural, inborn ability, that has never been impaired in any way, nor squelched by anyone else's perception of him. His eternal connection with The One Intelligence has never been blocked or broken. He shares in common with each of us the fact that he is an actual, individual, and unique spiritual expression of Love, Good, and Intelligence — and the interchange that takes place among all of us is as much a part of his experience as anyone else's.
>
> Spirit's "still small voice" is the same voice of Reason and Power that speaks to and through [your son] now. No loss or impairment he has been diagnosed as having in the brain can make any difference to that fact.
>
> If we look at the tyranny of a physical verdict that has been handed down to you, which says there is a lack of a corpus callosum, and if we accept that a corpus callosum is necessary for "normalcy," then we cannot meet the challenge.
>
> But we can choose to look deeper, at the spiritual reality. *Corpus callosum* means literally in Latin a "hardened" or "unfeeling" "body," a band of commissural fibers uniting the cerebral hemispheres. The *commissura* means "a joining together," and comes from the Latin, "to connect," "to send," or "entrust." Here's the idea of communication again — the "interchange" and "connecting passage" — which do not in reality reside in any particular location, namely in someone's grey matter in the skull!
>
> In Spirit, there is no location, no "in here" or "out there" — we are spiritual, not physical beings. Therefore [your son] *dwells within Love's connecting passage!* Regarding the meaning of

callosum as "hard" or "callous," you already know that he is just the opposite! I'm sure he has a natural trust and connection to others that is unique. This isn't based on whether a particular part of the brain is in some expected place or performing some predictable sequence.

Can he understand? Communicate properly? Progress normally? Yes, and likely go even farther than anyone ever expected!

After several years of prayer, speech therapy, and the patient work of loving parents and teachers, this child is not only now considered "normal" but "above average."

The eternal Law of Spirit has been obvious to many healers in ancient wisdom traditions. According to Webster's, *shamans* are healers who enter "an unseen world," "divining the hidden" in order to treat their patients. Michael Harner is a well-known anthropologist who wrote in *The Way of the Shaman* about his time spent in 1961 among the Conibo people of the Peruvian Amazon. Under the instruction of the Conibo shamans, in order to learn first-hand of their techniques, he took their hallucinogenic drink made from the *ayahuasca* plant. Soon he had the sensation that his body had become paralyzed, while he traveled a "spirit journey" through a world of mythological creatures. One of the startling experiences he recounts is that a group of dragon-like creatures crawled out of his spine. (Harner notes that although the beings were strikingly similar to DNA, at the time he knew nothing of DNA.) The creatures boasted that they had made all of creation, and that they resided in all of life. After the visions were over, Harner eventually regained his faculties, and finally ventured to tell one of the master shamans about his experience. The shaman nodded with recognition as Harner described the many places he'd been, and the amazing creatures he'd seen. When Harner got to the story about the dragon-like beings and their claim that they rule the universe, the shaman smiled, amused, and explained: "Oh, they're always saying that. But they are only the Masters of Outer Darkness."[45]

Compare the universal image of these evil, arrogant dragons, familiar Masters of the Outer Darkness in the shamanistic tradition, to the biblical picture of Satan as a serpent (in Genesis) or as a dragon (in Revelation).[46] From beginning to end, any way you look at it, materiality (including the so-called human mind) will always end up the same: existing only in that outer darkness *outside* the reality of Spirit's realm.

Are we material or spiritual? Whatever premise we choose, the corresponding conclusions will follow.

The Law of Spirit is always in effect, in every time, culture, and circumstance — from our ordinary comings and goings to the spinning of galaxies in the cosmos. We have only to obey Spirit's Law to stay healthy. The word *obey* comes from the Latin *ob* meaning "toward" and *audire* "to hear." Listen. When we listen to what our inner (spiritual) sense is telling us, what Spirit is *always* telling us — not to the bravado and threats of the fickle five senses — we will be protected. We will heal.

SPIRIT

SOUL

vitality

vital force

brisk

animation

esprit

oomph

vim

vigor

courage

dauntlessness

snap

substance

resolution

energy

power

fervor

enthusiasm

mettle

chutzpa

élan

temperament

lively

brio

LIFE

verve

zing

ardor

cojones

guts

character

pluck

zeal

might

strength

passion

heart

moxie

spunk

timbre

get-up-and-go

excitement

inspiration

set up

bright

vivacious

gingery

sharp

audacious

avid

resolute

metaphysical

numinous

elevated

rousing

saintly

rarefied

stamina

tone

psyche

elation

exhilaration

stimulation

alert

keen

fiery

peppy; peppery

high-hearted

bold

MIND

incorporeal

sacred

aesthetic sense

high-minded

dashing

light

ethereal

anima

THESE BLANK PAGES FOR YOUR NOTES AND
PRAYERS

ENDNOTES

THE LAW OF SPIRIT
ANNIHILATES MATERIALITY

1 Quoted from *Inner Reflections 2000* engagement calendar. Los Angeles: Self-Realization Fellowship, n.p.

2 *S&H,* p. 277:24 (only).

3 See *S&H,* p. 78:17–20. See also *Reinventing Medicine,* p. 28.

4 Words from the hit song by singer/songwriter John Mayer (Specific Harm Music [ASCAP]), "No Such Thing" (music by John Mayer and Clay Cook (Me Hold You Music [ASCAP]), from his CD album *Room For Squares.* New York: Columbia Records/Sony Music, 2001.

5 For further discussion see "The Truth About Failure," by Neale Donald Walsch. *Conversations with God Weekly Bulletin,* #8, August 27, 2002.

6 See *S&H,* p. 287:13–16.

7 See *S&H,* p. 339:11–19.

8 See *S&H,* p. 106:9–11 and p. 125:16–17.

9 See *S&H,* p. 475:28–31.

10 See *S&H,* p. 300:28–31; p. 361:16–18; p. 250:12–13.

11 See Eddy's discussions in *S&H,* pp. 300–301 and 515–516; and read *We Knew Mary Baker Eddy* (Boston: The Christian Science Publishing Society, 1979), p. 76–77.

12 See a further explanation of Genesis 1:1 in "Bible Notes," *The Christian Science Journal,* v. 117, no. 4, April 1999, p. 61.

13 *S&H,* p. 523:14–30. For two equally fascinating verse-by-verse analyses, see the "Genesis" chapter of *S&H,* as well as Elizabeth Cady Stanton's *Woman's Bible: The Original Feminist Attack on the Bible.* New York: Arno Press, 1974 (©1895–1898).

14 *S&H,* p. 171:4–11.

15 See *Peake's Commentary on the Bible,* General Editor Matthew Black.

Nashville, TN: Thomas Nelson, 1962, 1982, p. 774.

16 See *Webster's Collegiate Thesaurus.* Springfield, MA: G & C Merriam Company, 1976, p. 669.

17 The Bible contains a number of references to "the sons of God"; my idea of "the divine childhood" is an expansion of this idea in order to be all-inclusive. See Hosea 1:10, Romans 8:14, Galatians 4:6–7, and 1 John 3:1–2. See also *S&H*, p. 316:3–7, p. 226:20–21, and p. 517:30–518:4.

18 See *S&H*, p. 19:23–24.

19 *S&H*, p. 18:1–2. Eddy's definition of *atonement* has even made it into *Webster's* dictionary. For a fascinating explanation, read Chapter 2 of *S&H*, "Atonement and Eucharist."

20 From an interview with Laurance Doyle, PhD, astrophysicist at the Search for Extraterrestrial Intelligence (SETI) Institute, by Richard Moeschl, "Infinity and Individuality: Spiritual and Scientific Implications of Life Beyond Earth." Ashland, OR: RVTV, March 3, 2000. Hereinafter referred to as "Infinity and Individuality."

21 *Magical Mind, Magical Body.*

22 I thank astrophysicist Laurance Doyle, PhD, and my friend, Ron Ballard, healer, for sharing these observations.

23 *Magical Mind, Magical Body.*

24 See *S&H*, p. 374:12–13.

25 I thank my friend, Ron Ballard, healer, for sharing these ideas.

26 "Infinity and Individuality." In Laurance Doyle's discussion on the nature of Truth, he points out that it's no surprise that we call the uncovering of Truth "en*lighten*ment, not en*heavi*ment."

27 *S&H*, p. 258:13–15.

28 *S&H*, p. 248:13–29.

29 See *S&H*, p. 412:16–27.

30 *Magical Mind, Magical Body.*

31 See *Anatomy of the Spirit: the Seven Stages of Power and Healing* by Caroline

Myss. New York: Three Rivers Press, 1996, p. 35.

Ellen Curran, a medical nurse who uses guided imagery in the treatment of children suffering from chronic illnesses with remarkable results, also discusses Dr. Pert's work in Curran's book, *Guided Imagery for Healing Children and Teens: Wellness Through Visualization.* Hillsboro, OR: Beyond Words Publishing, 2001.

32 For an introduction to this engaging topic, see "A Body of Knowledge" by Stephen Kiesling, *Spirituality & Health,* v. 5, no. 1, Spring 2002.

33 *Magical Mind, Magical Body.*

34 *Healing and Christianity: The First Comprehensive History of Sacramental Healing in the Christian Church from Biblical Times to the Present* by Morton T. Kelsey, New York: Harper & Row, 1973, p. 303, 304. Hereinafter referred to as *Healing and Christianity.* (Kelsey is quoting here from Jung's *Modern Man in Search of a Soul,* ©1933.)

35 See *S&H,* p. xi:9–21.

36 *Healing and Christianity,* p. 332.

37 *Healing and Christianity,* p. 333.

38 See *Healing and Christianity,* p. 333, 342.

39 *Healing and Christianity,* p. 327.

40 *S&H,* p. 298:20.

41 *Spiritual Evolution,* p. 14.

42 See *S&H,* p. 207:20 and 268:6–9.

43 See *S&H,* p. 277–278, especially 277:24–278:14.

44 For an illuminating dramatization about an innocent victim of disease brought to trial and absolved, read Mary Baker Eddy's "allegory illustrative of the Divine Mind and of the supposed laws of matter and hygiene," *S&H,* p. 430:13–442:32.

45 *The Way of the Shaman: A Guide to Power and Healing,* by Michael Harner. San Francisco: Harper & Row, 1980, p. 7. Read chapter 1 for the full account.

46 See the Bible, Genesis chapter 1 and Revelation chapters 12 and 13.

3

Philosophers' stone:

something that has the power to transform; an
ultimate principle of spiritual regeneration.

TRUTH

Let's get real.

"Truth and Falsehood were bathing.
Falsehood came out of the water first
and dressed herself in Truth's clothes.
Truth, unwilling to put on the garments
of Falsehood, went naked."[1]

THE TRUTH ABOUT THE LIE

Seeking The Larger Truth

God is Truth. So we don't need to spend our lives vainly seeking a Truth that will remain just out of reach. And it's not that some religions have more truth than others, or that some people know more truth than others. Truly, we can't *have* Truth. On the contrary: Truth has *us*![2]

If any religious doctrine or leader, if any guru or teacher claims "Here's the Truth. We have it, and all these other folks don't" thus declaring outsiders to be condemned to damnation, etc. — that's a pretty small truth, isn't it? Let's seek a larger Truth. Let's talk about a Truth that is Infinity Itself: a Truth so big that It embraces everything — every religion, every species on Earth, plus all the galaxies and stars in the entire universe.

Truth is never limiting, but liberating. Jesus said, "you shall know the truth, and the truth shall make you *free*" (John 8:32). Resilient, Truth can *endure* all our questions.[3] Wherever we go, whatever we must do to find the answers to our own inner questions — either in our search for knowledge as a species throughout human history, or as individuals during a human lifetime — Truth abides. Truth will wait. Right here. Never someplace else, but ever-present, ever Truth-telling.

The Rule Of Inversion: Nothing Is Wrong

"Individuals are consistent who, watching and praying, can
'run, and not be weary; walk, and not faint,' [see Isaiah 40:31]
who gain good rapidly and hold their position, or attain slowly
and yield not to discouragement." — Mary Baker Eddy[4]

We seem to live in a world of opposites. We face a constant duality that appears never to be resolved. One Chinese cosmology describes this experience as the yin and the yang. This view accepts and even celebrates the opposites in our so-called material world. But if we look at existence as *spiritual* rather than material, we can see these opposites in a whole new light.

If we blindly accept the obvious chaos of constantly dueling opposites as all there is, we'll be agonizing forever in the morass of materiality, always up against impossible odds. Instead of battling through life oblivious to what's really going on, let's seek a higher Truth. We *can* get a glimpse of the larger picture — see what is spiritually true — where endless possibilities for good await. As Eddy says, "We must look deep into realism instead of accepting only the outward sense of things."[5]

We can also take advice from Jesus' parable: "[T]he kingdom of heaven is like unto a net, that was cast into the sea, and gathered of every kind: Which, when it was full, they drew to shore, and sat down, and gathered the good into vessels, but cast the bad away" (Matthew 13:47–48). Let's cast out the bad and keep the good. Let's throw out whatever doesn't work, and whatever doesn't make sense.

In other words, let's start from a spiritual premise: Reality is perfect. If this is the Truth, then absolutely anything is possible, and nothing is impossible!

Let's think about that phrase: "Nothing is impossible." *The truth is in the Word.* What are the messages we're saying to each other? What are we telling ourselves? The Truth is, Nothing *is* impossible, when we know the Somethingness of Good. Since Good is Infinite, then Nothing is outside of Infinity! Exactly. Nothing, as a concept, *is outside of Infinity,* that is, it's *outside of reality.*

Of course this is all a solecism in language, since by saying "nothing *is*" we are attributing essence to that which doesn't actually exist. But when we start with the statement *reality is perfect,* the blinders are suddenly off. The fun part is, it's all clear because now we can see that giving a name to *Nothing* is simply a way to describe *what isn't.*[6] We need a way to talk about what *doesn't* exist in order to understand the reality of what *does* exist. That's the new beauty of opposites revealed!

When we talk about such concepts as evil, disease, or death, these are simply *terms* we use to label what *isn't.* They are outside of Infinity, thus unreal. Nothing is outside of Truth. Thus there's nothing to fear! You see what happens when we examine the words we're using: "There's nothing to fear" means that whatever we *are* afraid of *is* Nothing. What a relief! When we awaken to this sublime fact, we see that all is well. The realization of this simple, profound Truth heals any circumstance, sometimes in an instant. When we know that what we fear is Nothing, we can easily replace fear with the Truth of Being. Thus fear isn't suppressed or ignored, but *destroyed.*

Here's an illustration: If you are filled with fear because you think you see a poisonous snake, but as you get a better look, you realize it's just a coiled rope, you breathe a sigh of relief. Your fear vanishes.[7] Focusing on the "snake" is called anxiety; therefore the continual refusal to accept a snake (the unreal) is necessary if we want to see the rope (the real).[8] When we understand this simple fact, and learn to seek the support of Divine help, we are able to see beyond what seems to be.[9] Then we understand the spiritual reality. This understanding heals physical disease and suffering of any sort.

In the chapter on the Law of the Spirit, we talked about there being only One Cause and Effect. There are so many things we worry about every day. But the Truth is, God causes all, and therefore All is Good. So it isn't foolhardy to say that nothing causes anything to happen! That is, Nothing *is* what seems to cause all the chaotic events of human experience.

For instance, we may think we know that of course cold weather causes the sniffles, that chopping onions makes us cry, or that falling can cause a broken bone, but these are observable "laws" which apply to a view of life as material, not to a discernment of the Science of Life as Spirit. When you are about to take a trip and your friend worries about you, you can truthfully say, "Don't worry, nothing is going to happen," and mean it. First, yes, Nothing *is* bound to happen. *Happen* literally means "to occur by chance." But in God (in Truth), all is harmonious, and never random. So, when Nothing happens (tragedy or good fortune), it will have no effect on you. Your true being is intact regardless of what happens.

Zero, The Point Of Departure

> "Let us rid ourselves of the belief that man is separated from
> God, and obey only the divine Principle, Life and Love. Here
> is the great point of departure for all true spiritual growth."
> — Mary Baker Eddy[10]

Let's look at all of this Nothing mathematically. *Zero* literally means "nothing," "the absence of all quantity," a "nonentity." Zero is the "point of departure in reckoning," which doesn't really exist except as a starting point that we must have in order to show *what is*. We wouldn't have any mathematics at all if it weren't for zero! Mathematicians, astronomers, and physicists couldn't describe anything without it. Try buying groceries without using zero. In other words, zero is *a term for what isn't,* but you can still use it to prove, to know, and to see *what is*.

The One Eternal Mind and material existence never unite; they are opposites.[11] Mind tells us only reassuring thoughts of Love, of Truth, of the reality that is permanent. Materiality, on the other hand, tells us what to fear, and how to worry about what may happen next. Which voice will we choose to listen to?

Here is another biblical parable about how to deal with opposites (see Matthew 13:24–30):

> Jesus told another parable, saying, "The kingdom of heaven is like a man who sowed good seed in his field. But while men slept, his enemy came and sowed tares among the wheat, and went his way. But when the blade was sprung up, and brought forth fruit, then appeared the tares also. So the servants of the householder came and said to him, 'Sir, didn't you sow good seed in your field? Then where did the tares come from?' He said to them, 'An enemy has done this.' The servants said to him, 'Do you want us to go then, so we can gather them up?' But he said, 'No; since while you gather up the tares, you might also root up the wheat with them. Let both grow together until the harvest: and in the time of harvest I will say to the reapers, "Gather together first the tares, and bind them in bundles to burn them: but gather the wheat into my barn."'"

This story is one way to explain the idea of separating the wheat from the chaff (tares), i.e., distinguishing between the good and the bad. The word *tare* is from the Middle English word for *weed*, which, ironically enough, is akin to the Middle Dutch word for *wheat* itself, *tarwe*. *Tare* also means "an undesirable element," "counterweight," and "that which is rejected" (from the Arabic, *tarha*).

Sometimes it can be tricky trying to recognize the wheat from the weed — that which is good from that which is not so good. Because of the counterfeit nature of evil, what *isn't* is often mistaken for what *is*. That's why Jesus admonishes us to be very careful not to be deceived. If we accept at face value this duality — a mixture of tares and wheat — this incorrect assumption will lead to incorrect conclusions every single time. Here are some examples of what results when we fail to separate the tares from the wheat (when we accept Nothing as Something):[12]

Assumption	Conclusion
1. Life and Intelligence — and thus our own life and mind — are separated from God.	Therefore, we are hopeless sinners, doomed to a life of suffering and cluelessness.
2. We are a mixture of the spiritual and physical, the mental and material.	Therefore, duality is a given, resulting in a perpetual struggle for balance that can never be achieved. We accept this as our natural condition(ing).
3. We'll always be a mixture of good and evil.	Therefore Evil and Good are constantly battling entities, while we're caught in the middle, a victim of capricious forces, buffeted from within and without.
4. Matter (namely the brain) is intelligence, and controls us. The corporeal body (our genes, etc.) constitutes identity.	Therefore, we must obey material laws, heredity, etc., and be subject to the pains and pleasures of matter. We are irreversibly bound to the cycle of birth, decline, and death.

On the other hand, suppose we take another look at the tares and wheat of existence, and this time choose to recognize only one reality (wheat), and to discard the counterfeit (tares). With this understanding, we know immediately that *the evil that seems to be* is only there to tell us what *isn't* true. Thus we can see the truth about Nothing:

Assumption	Conclusion
1. Life and Intelligence are One, and that One is Infinite.	Therefore, we are inseparable from God. We are the One Mind's thoughts. We are, each of us, a unique, cherished idea, connected to every other idea in Consciousness.
2. God is All — Life, Intelligence, Spirit. God is Infinity, leaving no room for materiality or physicality.	Therefore, materiality is illusion. The One reality is Infinite Spirit.
3. Good is the One Power, unopposed. We dwell only in Good; evil is a lie.	Therefore, regardless of how compelling evil may be, we cannot be impressed or persuaded by it. Because we are God's image (Mind's reflection), we are not a hodgepodge of the sometimes good, sometimes bad. We are whole and good.
4. We are not physical beings, but spiritual ideas. The body is a tangible expression of what we choose to think.	Therefore, whatever we entertain in thought is our experience.

Nothing means *none*. Literally *none* means "not one." Can it be any clearer than that? If there *is* only One, you can easily reject the ideas of "not one" and "no thing" as Nothing! This understanding is the line of demarcation between the real and the unreal.[13] As the Apostle Paul declares, "If God be for us, who can be against us?" (Romans 8:31).

The truth about the lie gets more and more fun the more you explore it. Be brave: We even need to be skeptical about our own skepticism; unless we're

involved, our thought can't evolve.[14] There's just no end to the discovery
— and bear in mind, the Truth survives our every inquiry.

Do you think your life is screwed up? Do you think you've made too
many mistakes, that you've been beaten down, broken? Think again. Repent.
Get your head around this one: Nothing is broken! Therefore there is no
brokenness. All is intact. Let's invite into our thinking the possibility that
the *opposite* of brokenness — integrity — *is* the reality. *Integrity* applies not
only to an adherence to moral values; it comes from the Latin word *integer*
meaning "entire," and "a complete entity." Integrity also means "wholeness,"
"soundness," "completeness," and "incorruptibility." If we are identifying
ourselves properly, we see our innate integrity, and we accept our inherent
wholeness.

My friend John Holmstrom, Hollywood documentary filmmaker, once had
a serious drinking problem. Here's how an understanding of the story of the
tares and the wheat helped to heal him of alcohol addiction and transformed
his life:

> I came across a passage from a letter that Mary Baker Eddy
> wrote to a student. It said: "You are *growing*. The Father has
> sealed you, and the opening of these seals must not surprise you.
> The character of Christ is wrought out in our lives by just such
> processes. The tares and wheat appear to grow together until the
> harvest; then the tares are *first* gathered, that is, you have seasons
> of seeing your errors — and afterwards by reason of this very
> seeing, the tares are burned, the error is destroyed. Then you see
> Truth plainly and the wheat is 'gathered into barns,' it becomes
> permanent in the understanding" (quoted in *We Knew Mary Baker
> Eddy,* p.90).

> I was determined to burn the tares and gather the wheat, so
> to speak. I decided to turn as wholeheartedly as I could to the
> study of God's healing law to resolve my business, drinking and
> personal problems....

> I began to see my true self was not that of a human struggling
> to be free of addictive, destructive practices; but in reality, my
> spiritual birthright provided me with a joyous freedom from lack
> or limitation of any kind. I had the right to be free of addiction
> to alcohol, lack of work, and depression. They were not of God
> and could not be part of me, as God's loving and loved child.

> One day, after several weeks of seeing myself in this light,
> I looked at a display of alcoholic beverages in a supermarket

and realized I was not battling with myself.... At first I couldn't believe it!.... I wondered if I was really healed or if the desire would return. Then I remembered this statement from *Science and Health*: "The drunkard thinks he enjoys drunkenness, and you cannot make the inebriate leave his besottedness, until his physical sense of pleasure yields to a higher sense. Then he turns from his cups, as the startled dreamer who wakens from an incubus incurred through the pains of distorted sense" (p. 322). I realized I had been awakened to the spiritual truth of my being, and the "tares [were] burned, the error [was] destroyed."

This healing has given me much-needed inspiration to apply these healing truths to all areas of my life.[15]

We've discussed the common view — that there are two sides to life: one full of loneliness and woe, tragedy and unfairness; the other transcendent, intangible, elusive, mostly out of reach. But this duality comes simply from not focusing! Here's what I mean. Notice when you first gaze through a microscope, and the view isn't lined up? You see two images. But when you adjust the focus, eventually you'll see the one true image. Our lives are just like that. We can look around and accept all this rubbish as just "the way life is" or, we can say "I won't accept this, I will not live in this scenario, I will only take in what is good and true and right, and discard the rest."

No longer do you need to accept the torture and fear you have allowed Satan — the lies about true existence — to throw at you all your life; it is all illusory, only a nightmare. The false picture holds no real weight — it is only the tares, a counterweight, an extra weight outside of the real picture. It is really just another Goliath. And he's standing there, an idiot full of bombast, signifying Nothing! And you are now ready to cut him to the quick with your well-placed slingshot.

We cannot run away from evil. We cannot ignore evil. If we do, we are only allowing it to get stronger. We already know this from our own experience: The more we try to deny suffering, the worse it will get. We must confront it: We must tell the Truth to every lie.[16] The Bible says, "Resist the devil, and he will flee from you" (James 4:7). You must face the evil and meet it head-on, as David did. Since knowing the Truth eliminates all fear, evil is exposed for what it is: Nothing, a shadow, a mist, a dream.

In the biblical account of Jesus' confrontation with the devil, Satan is as usual very deceptive, matching Jesus' quotes from Hebrew scripture, which Jesus knew well, to try to trip him up and persuade him to admit defeat (see Matthew 4:3–11):

And when the tempter came to Jesus, he said, "If you are the Son of God, command that these stones be made bread." But Jesus answered and said, "It is written, 'Man shall not live by bread alone, but by every word that proceeds out of the mouth of God.'"

Then the devil took him up into the holy city, and set him on a pinnacle of the temple, and said to him, "If you're the Son of God, cast yourself down: for it is written, 'He shall give his angels charge concerning thee: and in their hands they shall bear thee up, lest at any time thou dash thy foot against a stone.'" Jesus said to him, "It is written again, 'Thou shalt not tempt the Lord thy God.'"

Again, the devil took him up to an exceedingly high mountain, and showed him all the kingdoms of the world, and the glory of them; and said to him, "I will give you all these things, if you will fall down and worship me."

Then Jesus said to him, "Get thee hence, Satan: for it is written, 'Thou shalt worship the Lord thy God, and him only shalt thou serve.'" Then the devil left him, and, behold, angels came and ministered to him.

Some of the original words used for *Satan* or *devil* in the passage above are "accuser," "slanderer," and "liar."[17] This story of Jesus' experience teaches us how to dismiss effectively the devil's nagging voice of doubt and deception. The phrasing used in the second-to-the-last verse of this passage conveys Jesus' absolute imperative: Some translations have him saying "Begone!" Considered in the original Greek text, "Get thee hence, Satan" indicates the idea of a "sinking out of sight," or "fizzling out" (just like a snowflake to the flame in our snowglobe analogy, in the chapter on The Law of Principle).[18] Thus in reaction to Jesus' vehement protest, the devil didn't just hightail it out of there — he disappeared. Evil is a coward before Truth.[19] This description vividly illustrates Truth's promise: We are safe in God's care, in the assuredness of Principle, in the infinite realm of Harmony, always based in the solid footing of Spirit.

The Truth be told, there is no place where evil can get to us. So — don't go no place! If a lie is being flung at you, you don't have to catch it. If you do, you are no place! If evil is getting to you, you are no place! So *let go*! Remember your true identity in the divine childhood. Realign your thinking once again with Mind, the Truth of Being. You'll be back where you belong. Now you're really going *some*place!

Our word *some* actually comes from the Greek word for *same* — *homos* or *hama* — meaning "together" and "one"! As mentioned earlier, *none* means "not one." From the Old English, *none* also means "no one." The paradoxical reality remains: There is One I AM, and there is none else! Despite the multiplicity that *seems* to be, there is still just One.

So when we affirm in a loud voice, "Get thee hence, Satan! I am somebody!" we can feel how powerful that feels. We can *know* the Power that is fortifying each one of us. This is Truth defending us, Spirit comforting us, Principle guiding us.

You reflect the Infinite One — in your own unique way, and there's no one else who can fill your shoes but you. Isn't that astounding! You can't lose! There is nothing to lose: That is, all you have *to* lose (all you have to let go of) in order to realize the Truth is Nothing!

Truth requires our presence to be fully expressed and realized. And we need Truth to be fully who we are. This is easy to do, when we know we're inseparable from Truth. Once we are thoroughly convinced of this, nothing can stop us from experiencing harmony in every aspect of our lives.

By the way, the only thing that ever *can* stop you is Nothing. And now you already know what to do when that happens! When armed with Truth's slingshot, you can conquer seemingly overwhelming odds with one blow. You can turn around tragic circumstances. You will see that all of Life is miraculous. You will heal. Try it and see. Truth will wait.

Be Still

> "Pure and still, one can put things right everywhere under
> heaven." — Lao Tzu[20]

Try to look very closely at the bottom of a glass when you take a drink of water. There seem to be two glasses; but when you focus, holding the glass out in just the right spot, you'll see there's really only one glass. To see what I mean, try moving a glass in and out from your face, without moving your head, just adjusting your focus. You'll see the *one* glass whenever you are *still* and *focusing on what is*. In the same way, when a challenge rears its ugly head, be still, and know that you reflect the One; you are not separated from Truth. Remind yourself: There is one reality, not two. Re-Mind yourself: Evil cannot abide in the presence of Truth. Darkness cannot exist in the presence of Light.

An explanation of optics tells us that our eyes actually see everything upside down, but supposedly our brain translates the image to right side up. We have *two* eyes so that we can perceive depth. I was always happy as a young girl when I looked through my Viewmaster: Two pictures together would combine to become one three-dimensional image. As I've mentioned, binoculars and microscopes work on the same principle — two images, when we focus, become one.[21]

These simple lessons are additional illustrations of the fact that duality is an illusion. The duality that is commonly accepted as reality simply can't be. Any notion of something "other" — something "outside" of Allness — is just *what isn't*. What a wonderful comfort! This is not an abstract philosophical fabrication, but a practical, provable spirituality you can bring to every moment.

The more we see the spiritual reality of being, rejecting the lie, the more our experience will improve. That means all of humanity will improve. That means you. That means me. We will change reality. Not *ignore* the pain and sorrow, but *transform* it. Recognize it as powerless, illusion, counterfeit, old worn-out shoes we don't need to wear anymore. And *replace* the lie with the Truth. That's how prayer heals.

As mentioned before, stillness is vital in order to perceive the Truth. Otherwise, there is so much "noise" in our thinking and our *busy*ness — we're moving too fast to notice that the Truth of Being is right here all the time. A lake with choppy water can't properly reflect the surrounding landscape; but when the surface is completely still, the peaceful water reproduces a perfect image. In the same way, the more stillness we maintain, the more we will experience the underlying perfection. It makes sense that Psalm 23, one of the best prayers there is, tells us that God leads us "beside the still waters."

Spiritual teacher Gangaji describes this timeless message in the same elementary terms: "There is no separation between you and Truth."[22] Quoting her teacher, known as Papaji (H.W.L. Poonja, himself a student of Hindu holy man Ramana Maharshi), she says: "My teacher's message to you is, 'Stop.' 'Just be still.'"[23] Papaji also points out, she says, "'that the greatest obstacle, in fact the final obstacle, is the belief that there is an obstacle.'"[24]

Be still. Focus. And you'll be a better transparency for Truth.[25] Kathleen Noble, a licensed psychologist and Women's Studies Professor at the University of Washington who often writes about spirituality, uses an ancient Hindu metaphor to describe the process of spiritual focus:

> Imagine that the conscious or waking self is like water in a glass in the middle of the ocean. The ocean symbolizes the "Universe," or what some call "God," "Creator," or "All That Is." The glass represents the psychological lens through which we perceive both inner and outer worlds. The goal of spiritual intelligence

is to expand the borders of the glass while simultaneously increasing its translucence and permeability.[26]

Noble has published many of her studies on how people have applied what she calls their "spiritual intelligence" to overcome great adversity. Noble insists that "spiritual intelligence... never asks us to leave our good sense behind," but requires that we have "constructive skepticism."[27] If seeing that "all that is is holy" as 13th-century German mystic Meister Eckhart declares, then *learning to see,* Noble says, is absolutely crucial:

> *Seeing* is like contemplating a *Magic Eye* picture and learning to see beyond the illusion of its two-dimensionality. It takes time to see depth in what initially appears to be surface flatness, and a willingness to believe that it is there, even before the third dimension emerges. It takes practice to bring this dimension into focus and effort to bring one's focus back when it inevitably fades."[28]

Let's put into practice accepting this profoundly simple Truth: We're already free.

A friend told me she'd found a lump in her breast and asked me to pray for her before she went to the doctor. Below are some of the ideas I shared with her as part of our prayerful work together.

Lump means not only "totality," "aggregate," and "entire," it can also mean "a dull person," or even "beatings," "defeat," or "loss" (as in "taking lumps"). You might want to consider a lump showing up in your experience at this time. What does it mean to you? First of all, for certain it's *not* your fault, and you don't deserve it. Second, you don't have to accept it.

Start at the top with the spiritual reality: You are already totally and entirely good and pure and whole. If you've taken any beatings lately or if you have suffered any loss or defeat, you are stronger than any of these seeming setbacks, because each has provided you with lessons along the way to make you more full of wisdom, more able to conquer any enemy — because your nature and your being is and has always been Spirit, Love, Life, Truth. You are only becoming more fully so.

Breast has many other meanings besides a physical one — such as "meet boldly," "confront," "contend," "climb" and "ascend." You *can* meet the challenges before you with boldness and aplomb. You are not defeated. The *bosom* is "the seat of emotion and thought." So you might want to examine your thoughts: Throw out and let go of whatever comes into your thought that is negative, since those messages are self-defeating.

Start at the top: Keep the good out in front to guide you. *Breast* also means "front" or "face," as in "to be confronted by," "to have as a prospect or concern," or "to bring face to face." As you do this you probably already know what it is that you must face. Keep in mind that confrontation doesn't mean conflict. It means facing a fear, uncovering the problem, seeing there's nothing to be afraid of, and thus dismissing it. You can indeed "make a clean breast of" this problem, which although it may seem doubtful at the moment, or even alarming, has nothing to do with the real you and your true identity.

A number of days later, when my friend had the tests done, the doctor couldn't even *find* a lump.

No "What Ifs" — Know What Is

"And there arose a great storm of wind, and the waves beat into the ship.... And Jesus was in the back of the ship, asleep...: and they awoke him and said, 'Master, don't you care that we're about to perish?' And he arose, and rebuked the wind, and said to the sea, 'Peace, be still.' And the wind ceased, and there was a calm." (see Mark 4:37–39)

Face it: We have nothing to worry about. That's right. We really do have nothing to worry about. Anything that we *are* choosing to worry about *is* Nothing! All of evil's claims are crowded into nowhereness.[29]

This isn't wishful or nonsensical thinking, nor does it require human willpower. On the contrary. To be a "transparency for Truth" is to be still, to pray, to surrender. This kind of prayer means we are yielding to the One Mind, to the One Reality — recognizing our true identity. Step aside, give up the false picture of yourself, which blocks your path with evil's shadows. The sunshine of Truth, when given room, brings to light every answer you need.

Problems, conflict, disease, sorrow, worry, longing, anything discordant — these are real *only if* we are accepting them as real, mistaking them for reality. It's not that they are a figment of the imagination — they are solid conviction, they are powerful, *as long as* we invite them to stay in our consciousness. But if we sharpen the focus, realign our thinking, we can see instead what God is doing, what the One Mind is thinking: only Truth, only Spirit. "Rather than focusing on obtaining a quality we think we lack," says one *Christian Science Monitor* contributor, "we can become so familiar with our real, spiritual identity that what feels missing simply sharpens into view."[30]

When our view is clouded by worry, we can't focus on the spiritual reality. Worry is a blight upon us and creates perpetual gloom. The word *worry* comes from the Old High German *wurgen*, meaning "to strangle," and the Lithuanian *verzti*, "to constrict." Worry does indeed strangle us in evil's chokehold, as it also means "to harass by tearing, biting or snapping," to repeatedly "touch or disturb," "attack," "torment," or "afflict with mental distress or agitation."

How can we have mental distress, when we know that God is our mind? Mind imparts Truth to every individual. Each of us expresses this unchanging Principle, joy, Spirit. In the One Mind there can't be torment or struggle, since there's nothing outside of Infinite Good with which *to* struggle. There it is again: Nothing is outside of Good. How much time we waste, worrying about... Nothing!

Worry also involves anxiety, concern, and fear, including these shades of meaning: "to move, proceed, or progress by unceasing or difficult effort," "fret," "struggle," and a "nagging attention or effort." No doubt about it, worry definitely leads to no good — that is, worry leads us away from God!

When we worry, agonizing over a problem, large or small, we are always making something out of nothing. Worry is putting our trust in deception. Whenever we spend time analyzing what at its root is an impossibility, this rumination process only leads to more suffering. The word *suffer* can also mean to "allow" or "let"; one meaning is "to allow especially by reason of indifference." When we awaken and pay attention, what do we see that we are allowing into our experience? The answer to the endless merry-go-round of turning a problem over and over is to jump off. Turn away from suffering. Release it. Summarily dismiss it.

Psychotherapist Arline Curtiss, who has bipolar disorder (also known as manic-depression), and is also the daughter and brother of manic-depressives, treats her own disorder with what she calls Directed Thinking. After decades of struggle, Directed Thinking has brought her to sanity and equilibrium without medication. In her groundbreaking book, *Depression is a Choice,* she explains:

> Directed Thinking is the process by which, as an act of will, we choose particular and specific thoughts to switch the focus of our attention.... In this way we can escape the painful and traumatic feelings of depression,...while at the same time allowing this chemical imbalance to right itself through the

homeostasis brought about by new thoughts and actions; without the necessity of introducing outside chemicals.... The pain cannot think itself. We have to think it.... What we do not think about does not exist for us.... In reality, we can think only one thought at a time."[31]

Although Curtiss' method can't be fully described in one passage here, this excerpt indicates the powerful effectiveness of consistently choosing the Good in our thought.

As I mentioned in the chapter on the Law of Principle, to pray scientifically, we can't start with the problem — we must start with the solution. No "what ifs"! — know what is! Look into Truth first.

We can choose to rise above the chaos of a seemingly irresolvable mess. We can elevate our thought to the spiritual reality. Love is here: holding all, comforting all. The One Principle is still in power, ruling over all. Be still. Be unmoving. Don't be fascinated with that which is constantly changing and confounding you — disease, conflict, tragedy, sorrow, lack.

Truth answers when we call. Awareness is our guide. The One Mind — all the Intelligence of the universe — is our mind. There is nothing to be concerned about. Ah, there it is again. If we *are* worried or concerned, we're giving our time over to Nothing!

Concern has to do with a "marked interest or regard usually arising through a personal tie or relationship" and "an uneasy state of blended interest, uncertainty, and apprehension." But because each of us is God's child (Mind's reflection), the *only* real personal tie or relationship that exists is the unbreakable bond to Love — to our Father-Mother-Source. In our divine childhood, we need never attach ourselves to any so-called outside force — whether it seems to be the influence (negative or positive) of a family member, any other person, or any sort of difficulty. As the Buddha advises, we never need to attach nor engage; if we do, attachment will only lead to resistance, confusion, and suffering. As Gangaji so aptly puts it, "Reaction is misidentification."[32] When we recognize our *true* identity — realizing that there *is* no outside force — the murkiness of uncertainty melts away, revealing only purity. Then we can see that we're already perfect — never confused or disturbed — and always connected to God.[33] Thus there is no need to stay in the grip of anxiety or fear. Wriggle away. Be free. Freedom is your birthright as God's child.

David, that humble shepherd boy who later became Israel's king (with his own share of human frailties — see II Samuel chapter 11 for his sordid tale of adultery and murder), gives solid advice on this point, assuredly from his own experience: "Be still.... do not fret — it leads only to evil" (Psalm 37:7, 8, NIV).

So, what shall we worry about today? How about nothing? Choosing not to worry at all not only saves a lot of time, but we also become healthier — mentally, emotionally, morally, and physically. When the next crisis hits, you can immediately declare, *without irony*: "Nothing is *wrong*. All is well." This process isn't foolish denial, putting one's head in the sand; it is instead choosing not to react, choosing not to misidentify the situation. This affirmation of Truth is the first step to facing fear and seeing its vanity. This understanding of Truth is our doorway to the transformation of the circumstances: from darkness to Light, from chaos to calm, from sorrow to joy, from anger to forgiveness, from disease to health, from sin to wholeness, from resentment to Love. Truth is right, Truth is All. We are safe. We are OK.

The Human Condition(ing)

> "Listen to the silence / Feel your heart's alliance / Close your eyes / Breathe in the empty space / Welcome home to the sweet state of grace." — Johnny Elkins[34]

As Mary Baker Eddy writes, "materiality is the inverted image of spirituality."[35] Spirit is Truth; materiality is error. But, she explains, the fact that sin, disease, and death don't exist is no help to the sinner who wants to keep on sinning.[36] The sinner believes absolutely in the power of matter. This solid conviction solidifies matter and all material laws that go along with that belief. When we *awaken* to Truth, we can prove *for ourselves* the spiritual reality, and comprehend matter's powerlessness. Then and only then will the problems disappear into their native nothingness,[37] just as the devil dissolved in the Light of Jesus' rebuke.

A material belief, in all its manifestations, *reversed,* will be found to be Truth.[38] For example, the realization for me that the *opposite* of "manic-depression" is "calm exaltation" has often transformed my interactions with loved ones who suffer from this frequently exasperating mental illness. As I choose to hold to the power of the spiritual fact — rather than to be overwhelmed by any disturbing circumstances — my spiritual senses are strengthened, preventing an altercation or misunderstanding that might normally be expected to occur. When I choose not to react to the material picture and all its agonizing expectations, potential crises are averted without fail (and without medication). I continue to study this profound lesson: "The calm and exalted thought, or spiritual apprehension, is at peace."[39] This powerful prayer alone has diffused many a potentially explosive situation.

Remember the steps we can take in scientific prayer (see the chapter on the Law of Principle): 1. Declare the Absolute Truth; 2. *Affirm* the Truth and *deny* the lie; 3. Claim the healing as real and permanent. Here's another example of a healing that came from recognizing the spiritual truth of being by reversing the material picture. A mother was trying to comfort her young daughter, who had a high fever. The mother realized that the scene of a fearful, mortal mother rocking a sick child was *the exact opposite* of what was really going on. In her prayer, she took each aspect of the material picture and replaced it with a spiritual truth: "In place of a material child held in bondage to the fears of material parents, suppositional laws and medical beliefs was the spiritual child of God.... In place of a fearful human mother was the fearless spiritual expression of the one true Father-Mother God," and so on. She realized that simply by being the unopposed I Am That I Am, God was maintaining the health of her child — of God's own expression. She felt the fever leave the child instantaneously.[40]

Reality is only what we think it is — no more, no less. What are we inviting in? What are we admitting? What thoughts are we entertaining? Because all is consciousness, whatever we accept is what is real; whatever we reject will leave our experience.

Psychologist Jeanne Achterberg, director of research and rehabilitation science at the University of Texas Health Science Center in Dallas, tells the story of a woman with a massive brain tumor who was comatose and paralyzed upon admission to a hospital; the woman had surgery to "debulk" the tumor but was sent home without radiation treatment or chemotherapy since the doctors considered her so close to death. To their surprise, she improved each day and within sixteen months showed no trace of the cancer. How did this happen? Although the woman was intelligent, she wasn't very educated and really didn't understand the significance of the word *tumor* nor the supposed death sentence that came with it. "Hence, she did not believe she was going to die and overcame her cancer with the same confidence and determination she'd used to overcome every other illness in her life."[41]

Remember the snowglobe analogy. Shall we grab onto whatever assumptions may be floating by? We can go through life captivated by the false education we've inherited in our particular era, location, family, and culture. We can accept the paradigm of materialism, and live under its spell any time we choose. We can readily accept world opinion, parents', friends', politicians', or the media's opinions, etc., but they'll always be in flux with the ebb and flow of human belief. Everyone once knew the earth was flat. An eclipse used to be the portent of doom. Weather conditions were the sports of the gods. Diseases and hereditary ailments tend to come and go according to fashion and commerce. As a human community on this particular planet we're still often bitterly divided, focused on the false sense of separation —

separated from whatever we've labeled as "right," and separated from each other by race, religion, class, etc.

However, we can instead explore the new paradigm of the new millennium. Gangaji again directs us to hold to That Which Does Not Move, instead of being fascinated by everything swirling and changing around us.[42] "Overthrow the conditioning of the human mind,"[43] advises Alan Lithman, who has written extensively on the evolution of consciousness. Each of us, he says, possesses all knowledge already, "through identity, not acquisition."[44]

Live without fear or worry, because you know Life is eternal and limitless. Invite into your thought the Truth — what the One Mind is thinking, not the "what ifs" of common thinking.

Of course, we all feel lost and alone at one time or another. But when we feel lonely, we can stop and be still. We can re-Mind ourselves: We can't ever be isolated or separated from Truth.

Instead of being *alone,* you are "all one," which is exactly what the word *alone* means. Loneliness is impossible in All-One-ness.

If you still think something's missing in your life, look at what you are really saying about yourself. The word *miss* has these shades of meaning: "fail" "escape," "avoid" "lack," "mutable," and "loss." In the chapter on The Law of Spirit, we examined the meanings of *sin* — including "to miss the mark" or "to lead astray." Don't take that dark road. Go back to Truth, and *know what is.* Our true nature is not sinful, but good. Our true identity is pure. At moments when we think our true self is *missing,* then we're "absent from the place where it is expected to be found," "lost," "not present when called." This mental darkness is of our own making![45] But the Light is still on; God never stops telling us the Truth.

So, making something out of Nothing truly is missing the point! Instead, go out and be Somebody. Nobody is stopping you! That's right. Nobody and Nothing (Satan, evil, doubt, and misidentification) are the only things keeping us from being who we really are. We don't need those hassles. Whenever we let go of Nothing, to which we so often grant so much weight, a great burden is lifted.

Kicking Satan's "But..."!

"For with God nothing shall be impossible." (Luke 1:37)

Have fun with this recognition of your innate freedom! Gather your ammunition for the next round. As we add more smooth stones to our bag, we're better prepared to meet each challenge and dispel fear as nothing:

With God, nothing is impossible: The existence of Nothing is impossible!

Nothing is the matter. Nothing is matter. Nothing is wrong.

Nothing is bothering me.

I'm worried over nothing.

Nothing's going to happen. But Something is in control!

Nothing can be lost. But Something is always Somewhere!

Nothing can stand in my way. Something is lighting my path!

Nothing's going to stop me from doing what's right.

There is Nothing to hold on to — so let go of it!

On the blank pages at the end of this chapter, add your own discoveries to this list.

When life gets you down, stop. Be still. Pray. You *can* snap yourself out of the mesmeric mire of obsessiveness. And, thank God, this doesn't require willpower (willpower actually leads us away from spiritual understanding).[46] What is required of us is awareness — an honest yielding to Truth. No matter how grave the problem, Truth gives us the ladder we need to get out of the hole we're in. Each of us will be supplied with whatever we need in order to recognize again *what is.*

The devil (evil, deception) will relentlessly insist "yes...but..." trying to break our resolve. When we give in, we slide right into hell on our "buts."[47] Instead, let's kick Satan's "but"! — just *stop* at "yes!" and stand firm. When we stop at "yes!" we stand — steadfast, sure, triumphant, even if all odds are against us. Just like David facing Goliath. As God's children we can't lose.

You may want to read some parts of this chapter a few times to get what I'm driving at. Read out loud if you have to!

TRUTH

veracity

precision

authentic

veritable

candid

sincere

the heart of the matter

fact

precision

frankness

ideal

transcendence

integrity

original

credo

proof

rightness

genuine

PRINCIPLE

gospel (good news)

the Gospel

reality

real

observant

accurate

indisputable

honest

actuality

standard

obvious

exactness

pure

bona fide

basic

validity

motto

belief

certainty

main idea

crux

substance

acceptable

faith (Icelandic: *tryggth*)

natural

gist

essence

revelation

tenet

conviction

verity

fundamental

core

THESE BLANK PAGES FOR YOUR NOTES AND PRAYERS

ENDNOTES

THE TRUTH ABOUT THE LIE

1 Source unknown.

2 "Infinity and Individuality."

3 This introduction on Truth comes from some of the ideas shared by Laurance Doyle, "Infinity and Individuality."

4 *S&H,* p. 254:2–6.

5 *S&H,* p. 129:22–24.

6 For further clarification of the counterfeit nature of evil, read *Unity of Good*, especially "A Colloquy" between Good and evil, p. 21–26.

7 Note the classic example from preeminent Advaita Vedanta philosopher Sankara (c. 788–820 CE), of a rope on a path believed to be a snake, an error arising from *avidya* (ignorance) of *Brahman* (the ultimate Truth, the One Spirit, or the Absolute). For further reading on the subject see *World Religions,* pp. 17, 21–22, 115, 163, and 854–855.

A similar allegory regarding the belief of a snake is also applied in practical terms in a discussion about the process of healing through prayer, in: "Caring Enough to See Only the Real," by Patricia Tupper Hyatt. *The Christian Science Journal,* v. 105, no. 2, February 1987, p. 1–3.

8 See *Depression is a Choice: Winning the Battle Without Drugs* by A. B. Curtiss. New York: Hyperion, 2001, p. 22. Hereinafter referred to as *Depression is a Choice.*

9 See *One Day at a Time in Al-Anon.* New York: Al-Anon Family Group Headquarters, Inc., 1968, 1988, p. 148.

10 *S&H*, p. 91:5–8.

11 See *S&H,* p. 282:11–12.

12 See also Eddy's "Erroneous postulates," *S&H,* p. 91:22–92:8.

13 See *S&H,* p. 505:21–22.

14 "Bridging Science and Spirituality: An Inquiry into the Evolution of

Consciousness" a lecture given by Alan Lithman at The Horizon Institute, Southern Oregon University, Ashland, Oregon, May 17, 2000. Hereinafter referred to as "Bridging Science and Spirituality."

15 "I Had the Right to Be Free of Addiction," in *Healing Spiritually: Renewing Your Life Through the Power of God's Law.* Boston: The Christian Science Publishing Society, 1996, p. 315-317. All parentheticals and italics are in the original. Hereinafter referred to as *Healing Spiritually.* (The quote Holmstrom mentions reading is from *We Knew Mary Baker Eddy.* Boston: The Christian Science Publishing Society, 1979, p. 90.)

16 See *S&H*, p. 418:28–29.

17 See Dummelow, p. 632–634.

18 In *Strong's*, on p. 93 of the *New Strong's™ Concise Dictionary of the Words in the Greek Testament with their Renderings in the King James Version,* the Greek word is *hupago.* "Begone, Satan!" is the translation used in both the New English Bible and the Moffatt Bible. *Begone* also means "be off."

19 See *S&H*, p. 368:4–5.

20 From *Tao Te Ching: The Classic Book of Integrity and the Way* by Lao Tzu. Translated, annotated, and with an afterword by Victor H. Mair. Part of the *Mystical Classics of the World* series. New York: Book-of-the-Month Club, 1998, p. 13.

21 For more ideas on this subject see *S&H*, p. 111:14–18 and p. 301: 24–29.

22 Gangaji, "Vigilance" lecture broadcast on Free Speech TV, cable access, March '00. Hereinafter referred to as "Vigilance."

23 *The Gangaji Foundation 2000.* Novato, CA: The Gangaji Foundation, p. 4. Hereinafter referred to as *Gangaji Foundation 2000.*

24 *Gangaji Foundation 2000,* p. 1.

25 See *S&H*, p. 295:16–24.

26 *Riding the Windhorse: Spiritual Intelligence and the Growth of the Self* by Kathleen Diane Noble. Cresskill, NJ: Hampton Press, 2001, p. 45. Hereinafter referred to as *Riding the Windhorse.*

27 *Riding the Windhorse,* p. 127.

28 *Riding the Windhorse,* p. 122.

29 "Neither Villains Nor Victims," by Paul Stark Seeley. *The Christian Science Journal,* v. 61, no. 2, February 1943, p. 107.

30 "My New Year's Resolution," *The Christian Science Monitor,* December 31, 2002, p. 23. [No author's name given]

31 *Depression is a Choice,* p. 26, 158, 175, and 235.

32 Gangaji, public meeting, Ashland, OR, The Windmill Inn, October 4, 2000. Hereinafter referred to as Gangaji public meeting.

33 See also *S&H,* 306:18–29.

34 Words taken from "Listen to the Silence," a song in the musical *Leap! A Musical Quest,* by Mark Henderson (The Raj Publishing [ASCAP]) and Johnny Elkins, which premiered in Santa Barbara, CA, by Access Theatre, in 1995.

35 *S&H,* p. 572:10–11.

36 See *S&H,* p. 339:11–19.

37 See *S&H,* p. 91:9–15.

38 See *Miscellaneous Writings,* p. 60:28 and *S&H,* p. 129:7.

39 *S&H,* p. 506:11–12. For an authenticated testimony of a healing of manic-depression through prayer alone, see "I Could No Longer Accept the Verdict of a Lifetime of Mental Illness," in *Healing Spiritually,* p. 280–282.

40 "But Why Does Evil *Seem* to Be?" by Patricia Tupper Hyatt, *The Christian Science Journal,* v. 102, no. 1, January 1984, p. 17–20.

41 *Holographic Universe,* p. 85. See also Jeanne Achterberg's book, *Imagery in Healing.* Boston: New Science Library, 1985.

42 "Vigilance."

43 "Bridging Science and Spirituality."

44 "Bridging Science and Spirituality."

45 See *Miscellaneous Writings,* p. 355:18–20.

46   See *S&H,* p. 144:14–22.

47   From Marian English, "Spiritual Healing in the 21st Century," a public talk given in Ashland, Oregon, Ashland Springs Hotel, May 22, 2005.

4

Touchstone:

a test or criterion for determining
quality or genuineness.

Let's be practical.

> "Every great scientific
> truth goes through three stages.
> First, people say it conflicts with the Bible.
> Next, they say it has been discovered before.
> Lastly, they say they have always believed it."
> — Louis Agassiz, Swiss-born American
> naturalist and opponent of Darwin's
> theory of evolution, 1807–1873[1]

THE LAW OF LIFE CONQUERS DEATH

Evolution

Is life in a physical body, DNA, or the brain? Do we cease to be when the heart stops beating, or when the brain stops functioning, as conventional medicine insists? Are we mere mechanical random biological collisions that result in the natural selection of species throughout a material history?

Our intuition and inner experience tell us over and over that *God is our life,* not the material counterfeit picture. But how can we understand Life logically, and make this understanding practical? There *can* be scientific reasoning behind all this. First, we begin from the correct premise. Once we establish that there really is only Mind, we understand that One Intelligence is governing the universe.

As we've already talked about, physical scientists are themselves beginning to approach this conclusion. Biologist Arne A. Wyller says there is a "Mind Field," an Intelligence behind the evolution of life, precluding Darwin's theory of chance and natural selection.[2] He points out that there is actually no mathematics nor natural science in Darwinism.[3] Such scientists, who feel Darwin's view is insufficient, are called *vitalists* rather than materialists: Instead of taking a mechanistic view of life, they say that a life principle is living in and through matter. This idea really goes all the way back to Aristotle (384–322 BC) in the Golden Age of Greek philosophy. Plato, another philosopher of that time (428–348 BC) also pointed us in the right direction: He theorized that we live in a world of ideas, and that "material forms are imperfect renditions" of reality.[4]

Now let's go *beyond* both the vitalists' and the materialists' view, since they each still contain the duality of Spirit vs. matter. "Faith and science are by no means incompatible," says Owen Gingerich, professor of astronomy and the history of science at the Harvard-Smithsonian Center for Astrophysics. We are asking the wrong question, he says, when we argue over Creationism vs. Evolution. "The real question is, Accident or Purpose?"[5] Russell Stannard, professor of physics at England's Open University, insists that any reservations on the part of any physical scientist to explore religion are groundless, holding that it is "a mistaken belief that science has somehow disproved religion."[6] Carl Friedrich von Weizsäcker, physicist and philosopher awarded the Templeton Prize for Progress in Religion in 1989 concludes: "Theology, finally, is the attempt to express rationally what is being experienced and sought."[7] Indeed, throughout the 20th century the work of many physicists moved towards what they call a Theory of Everything that would explain all aspects of reality in one unified mathematical scheme.[8] And isn't this a spiritual quest? Physicist Paul Davies even goes so far as to say that science actually offers a surer path than religion does in the search for God.[9]

Recall from the chapter on Mind that *theology* literally means "The Word of God." Let's go back to the line in Genesis (1:3) that probably just about everyone knows by heart, God's first words, "'Let there be light': and there was light." It's worthwhile to point out here that scientists have shown that light is utterly unique. Light is not only simultaneously a particle and a wave; at rest it has no mass, weight or electric charge, yet it is a vital ingredient in all atoms and therefore in all life.[10] Quantum physicists explain that electrons — or any of an atom's smaller particles — are just *terms* we use to talk about something that, as it turns out, has *no dimension,* but is instead a manifestation of consciousness.[11]

All these scientists are discovering scientifically what Plotinus, a 3rd-century Roman philosopher, declared: He said that the Light is an Intelligence by which The One sees Itself.[12] So this information certainly isn't new. Light is Life. If Life is God, and we are God's offspring, then we are *Light's reflection.* Now this truth is plain, and sets us free to see that Life is eternal, not material nor temporal, nor subject to death or randomness of any sort. There simply is no matter. Put another way, matter isn't what we once thought it was. In the late 19th century, Mary Baker Eddy wrote:

> Atomic action is Mind, not matter. It is neither the energy of matter, the result of organization, nor the outcome of life infused into matter: it is infinite Spirit, Truth, Life, defiant of error or matter. Divine Science demonstrates Mind as dispelling a false sense and giving the true sense of itself, God, and the universe; wherein the mortal evolves not the immortal, nor does the material ultimate in the spiritual; wherein man is coexistent with Mind, and is the recognized reflection of infinite Life and Love.[13]

A mnemonic I like to use comes from spiritual teacher John-Roger: we are LIGHT, i.e., *Living In God's Holy Thoughts*.[14] Jesus said we are "Children of Light" the moment we decide to believe in the Light (see John 12:36).[15] Paramahansa Yogananda (1893–1952), the venerable yogi from India who founded the Self-Realization Fellowship in America, would likely tell us that Jesus was actually speaking literally: "He who knows himself as the omnipresent Spirit is subject no longer to the rigidities of a body in time and space.... *The law of miracles is operable by any man who has realized that the essence of creation is light*."[16] When Jesus said "The light of the body is the eye; if therefore thine eye be single, thy whole body shall be full of light" (Matthew 6:22), I think what he was saying is that when we totally give up on viewing life as ruled by duality, and instead choose the one and only spiritual reality, we will awaken to the fact that our bodies are *not* material. With Jesus' explanation, the Divine proclamation from the Bible's first chapter of Genesis, "Let there be light" takes on a deeper meaning, and dispels darkness for all time.

Ray Kurzweil, preeminent expert on artificial intelligence, predicted in 1999 that in less than 100 years there won't be "any clear distinction between humans and computers." He also said that the term *life expectancy* will no longer be "a viable term in relation to intelligent beings." These scenarios are provocative and indeed possible.[17] But super brains or bionic bodies still have nothing to do with what Life truly is.

As we've already established, consciousness is not located in a particular place called the brain. Paul Pietcsch, a biologist at Indiana University, conducted a series of over 700 operations in which he "sliced, flipped, shuffled, subtracted, and even minced the brains of his hapless subjects [salamanders], but always when he replaced what was left of their brains, their behavior turned to normal." In another experiment, neuropsychologist Karl Lashley taught mice to go through a maze, and then parts of their brains were removed; no matter which parts were taken, the mice still remembered the route.[18] Rupert Sheldrake, well-known biologist and vitalist, has challenged the mechanistic worldview with his theory that "morphic fields" create a "collective memory," i.e., a "morphic resonance" that transcends space and time among species. For example, in one experiment after rats of a particular breed were taught a specific trick in California, rats of that same breed elsewhere in the world were able to learn that same trick more quickly. Sheldrake has also conducted more complex learning experiments with humans.[19]

These are only a few illustrations that show the increasing evidence that Life is One Mind (some might call this One Intelligence the Cosmic Mind or the Christ Consciousness) — and that we are all connected as Its ideas.

These examples also teach us about the powers we so often give to cultural and social conditioning. Yet as soon as we become aware of any mistaken material patterns, we can dismiss them. We can put aside the shackles of limitation handed to us by erroneous education regarding disease, age, and death: They are illusions — only lessons in wrong thinking that can be corrected. When we recognize the Law of Life, the so-called physical laws of matter can't have any validity. It is then easy to say "yes" to Truth and "no" to the fallacy.

Interestingly enough, Kurzweil calls the essence of intelligence "the purposeful destruction of information." A neuron in the human brain either fires or it does not fire; a computer reads either a one or a zero. Each simple yes-or-no result creates each piece of data. In other words, our intelligence evolves by rejecting useless information.[20] Remember, when we recognize what isn't, we can easily recognize what is.

Michael Talbot, author of *The Holographic Universe* and *Beyond the Quantum*, calls matter "a kind of habit.... The laws of physics are not set in stone, but are more like [the way]... our own habits and deeply held convictions are fixed in our thoughts."[21] We are "at heart just images, holographic constructs, created by thought," says Dr. Ian Stevenson, professor of psychiatry at the University of Virginia Medical School.[22] Dr. Deepak Chopra explains that in every second of our existence we are creating a new body — because the body is not made of matter, but instead is a "frozen moment of attention" or "field of awareness" constructed by our thoughts. Our bodies respond to whatever thoughts we accept as true.

Dr. Larry Dossey calls the word *patient* as misleading as the word *particle*. We are not separate biological units, he says, but unanalyzable dynamic patterns and processes.[23] Our health or sickness is based on our beliefs — the beliefs we decide to take in from society, from family, from friends, from the media, from the medical community, from other experts, and so on. What beliefs will you choose? Which ones will you discard?

Again considering the snowglobe analogy, which habitual thinking shall we choose? Will we choose the outgrown superstition that each of us is a material human, subject to fleshly birth, decline, and death? Or will we dare to embrace the spiritual reality — that each of us is an idea of the One Divine Mind, eternally present, ever-unfolding? Think of it: a complete *idea* dwelling in the Light of Intelligence can't be harmed by *thoughts* of disease. Our individuality and identity reflect God's image and likeness. That's what it all comes down to: Each of us is a unique and infinite expression of Life itself. When we can really see this fact completely, we will not experience life as material: We will not age, nor will we experience death.

The evolution that's really going on is not biological, but spiritual.[24] Thus the evolution of human consciousness will eventually yield to a universal awareness of our true spiritual identity. Hundreds of years ago it was common knowledge that the earth was the center of the universe. Over time, this geocentrism yielded up to a better idea — that the sun was actually in the center of an entire solar system, which was found to be a small part of a greater galaxy. Gradually our knowledge about the universe grew, getting us "out of the way" so that we could, as astrophysicist Laurance Doyle puts it, "participate in the universe." Doyle, an astrophysicist at the SETI (Search for Extraterrestrial Life) Institute in California, says it's now time for another "unselfing": He explains that we're getting to the point where we could consider the possibility that "maybe molecules aren't life.... Maybe what's really sacred is the Law of Life that underlies that expression." He describes our current paradigm shift: "We're making a transition from matter in the middle to consciousness in the middle. We're making a transition from things to thoughts — to ideas being the substance of the universe."[25] Once we all agree to awaken to this reality, our understanding of the universe as a species will be ready to change again. This evolution of Intelligence is a never-ending process of Life's progress.

Mind Over Matter

"Row, row, row your boat

gently down the stream.

Merrily, merrily, merrily, merrily,

Life is but a dream."

When we go through the experience we call human life — birth, decline, death — what is it? Because it is perceived as matter, which doesn't really exist, it is a dream. The suppositional human mind or human experience as material is defined by Mary Baker Eddy as "mortal mind," "material consciousness" or the "Adam dream," and by Apostle Paul as the "carnal mind," "the flesh," or "the world." The striking term "monkey mind" has been used as well (signifying the constant background chatter of human thought).[26] We could also call it the "body mind" (in which we perceive the body and mind as separate and material, as opposed to the actual "Mind body," in which we accept the reality of the body as spiritual, within the One Consciousness). The Vedas call it the "physical mind" (in which we perceive separateness and doubt) or *maya* (Sanskrit for "illusion" or "ignorance"). Don Miguel Ruiz, a *nagual* (shaman) from the Eagle Knight lineage in Mexico, explains that according to ancient Toltec wisdom, the human mind is in a fog called *mitote*: "Your mind is a dream where a thousand people talk at the same time, and nobody understands each other. This is the condition of the human mind — a big *mitote*... [in which] you cannot see what you really are."[27] This *mitote* fog points to the same "mist" that arises from the ground in Genesis 2:6–7 in the Bible (see the chapter on the Law of Spirit), which introduces the counterfeit story of creation. In this Adam dream there is no escape from the self-imposed suffering of mortal life — unless we wake up.

Over a century ago, when Eddy coined the now-familiar phrase "Mind over matter," she wasn't talking about human willpower overcoming adversity; she was referring to the supremacy of the One Mind (the One Life) over the false concepts of sin, sickness, and death. Once these lies are revealed for what they really are — Nothing — the mind and body respond and are healed.[28]

Jesus is probably the most famous instance of a person proving that Mind over matter is possible, since he resurrected after death. In the Jewish tradition the Old Testament also tells the story of Enoch who ascended, i.e., "walked with God" (see Genesis 5:24 and Hebrews 11:5). Throughout history there can be found numerous instances that point to the spiritual reality of Life. In common thinking, however, we choose to disregard them all as "miracles" or "phenomena" instead of recognizing these events as glimpses of God's Law of Life — *of what really is*, governing all the time.

The "miraculous" or "supernatural" is indeed supremely natural.[29] In 1982 an English physician working in Pakistan was visited by a 35-year-old pregnant Pakistani woman. Eight months along, she was suffering from abdominal pain and some bleeding. At the hospital she began bleeding heavily, so the doctor delivered the baby by Cesarean section. The baby was fine, but the bleeding continued. Soon even a blood transfusion was not going to be enough to replenish the woman's blood. With no other options, the doctor turned to God: "We prayed with the patient after explaining to her about Jesus in whose name we prayed for her before the operation, and who was a great healer. I also told her that we were not going to worry." Two days later her blood finally began to clot, and ten days later she was home with the baby. Ten to twelve pints of blood are necessary to replenish the average human body, and the doctor had been certain that the woman had lost more than her total blood volume. Since humans aren't capable of producing new blood fast enough in the case of such catastrophic blood losses, one can only conclude that the patient's new blood "must have materialized out of thin air."[30] The Truth is, Life Itself is the only Power, neutralizing any beliefs about a required quantity or quality of blood to sustain It.

When I myself was pregnant, at the start of one particular office visit the doctor was alarmed at a high blood-pressure reading. The nurse said she would wait ten minutes and take another reading. During the wait, I held to the spiritual fact that there can be no legitimate pressure on me if God is the Only Power, exerting only the force of Good. I also recalled Eddy's idea that the only so-called "pressure" we ever live under is Paul's "apostolic command" to come out of the material world and be separate.[31] As I relaxed and considered this spiritual fact, I chose to reject the notion of blood pressure (a so-called material law) and looked only to "apostolic pressure." The next reading was so much lower, all the nurses in the office were talking about it, astounded.

There are testimonies everywhere to the effectiveness of Mind-healing. These answers to prayer are *not* examples of faith healing, but of healing that comes through the understanding and application of the Law of Life. These healings come to people of all faiths and persuasions whenever they catch a glimpse of our spiritual reality.[32]

When we awaken to Life's spiritual reality, we can heal any situation through prayer. With practice, we can learn to reject automatically the diseased, aging, or dying picture and replace it immediately and consistently with the correct one — whole, growing, progressing.

Re-Mind yourself of who you are, of what is. And all is well — for yourself, for your loved ones, for the community, for the world, for the cosmos, for the One Self. This is Self-realization: This is scientific prayer.

Life's A Joy, Then You Ascend

"The good cannot lose their God, their help in times of trouble. If they mistake the divine command, they will recover it, countermand their order, retrace their steps, and reinstate [God's] orders, more assured to press on safely. The best lesson of their lives is gained by crossing swords with temptation, with fear and the besetments of evil; insomuch as they thereby have tried their strength and proven it; insomuch as they have found their strength made perfect in weakness, and their fear is self-immolated." — Mary Baker Eddy[33]

The unfair and confusing mortal existence of birth, decline and death is often spoken of in derogatory terms, such as the popular saying, "life's a bitch, then you die." In the common way of thinking about life, that's certainly the way it looks. The human life cycle doesn't offer much rhyme or reason, and it never will. But if you're awake to the Truth about Life, and you know there is no life in matter — what joy this understanding brings! Once we see that in actuality "Life is a joy, then you ascend," we can look at every challenge in our experience without fear. Since we live only in the realm of Mind rather than in a material realm, all that ever needs to change to solve any problem is our thinking.

Deepak Chopra explains: "Every single problem that you have in your life is the seed of an opportunity for some greater benefit."[34] I look at it this way: When we have trials in our lives, they don't ever come from God. God doesn't even *know* about problems! Life *can't know* anything about death! So all problems come from "mist-taken" thoughts — foggy, unfocused thoughts that can be discarded and replaced with the Truth. The word *problem* means "obstacle" and "to throw forward" — and it actually originates in the Greek word for *devil* (*diabolos*), which means "to throw across" and "slanderer." When obstacles are thrown across our path, these are life's curveballs. The good news is, they are tests we can always ace! Or, if we don't quite succeed, we can know for certain that at least we will always get a passing grade! So we can rejoice in our trials, because just like story problems in math, algebra problems, or geometry proofs, each has an answer that already exists. Eddy says matter-of-factly, "Trials are proofs of God's care."[35] There is a mathematical, Scientific rule to Life that applies, and all we have to do is solve it. Since our mind is God's Mind, we already have the solution.

Trials are ways we can prove to ourselves and to others that God exists and is indeed ruling over all. Any *trial* as defined in the dictionary is a *test*, "that with which something is compared for proof of genuineness," and "refinement (as gold from lead, or purifying one's character)." Likely you're familiar with the expression "what doesn't kill you makes you stronger," and surely we prove that one all the time, even if we think that life is merely mortal. But when we know that Life is eternal, then we know there is no risk of death in the first place. We were never born into a mortal existence, we don't live in a material realm, and we don't die out of matter either.

Consider: A *test* can also be a "touchstone" or "standard" by which we can measure our progress, each challenge bringing us a little closer to a full spiritual understanding and awareness of Life. Each test that comes is actually one we're ready to take, because God isn't the taskmaster. The Bible says that God can't be tempted with evil, nor can God tempt anyone; people are tempted by their own lusts and enticed away from the right path (see James 1:13–17). Since it's error, not God, that lands us in whatever mess we're in, God is here to take us out of it — whenever we're willing. Refinement can take time, patience, a giving up of some aspect of our cherished materiality. A material sense of existence is cherished only because it's our habit of thinking — it's what we're comfortable with. As we wake up to the spiritual reality our comfort level changes, until we're ready to make the next move.

We can see examples of this character refinement as a species. We've gradually awakened to the injustices of slavery, monarchy, sexism, bigotry of every sort, global warming, etc. We can choose to step up to the tasks of effecting positive change, even in the face of seemingly impossible odds. In awakened consciousness, we can begin to see that in any battle we fight — no matter how tenacious the enemy, be it physical, mental, financial, etc. — we are actually striking out against error. Individually and collectively, we are simply struggling within our own clouded view. As we realize that the opposition is powerless, since Infinite Life can have no opposite, we can more easily blast away the misty fog, to reveal the Truth that's always here.

So no matter how big the battle may seem, even if it's bigger than Goliath, it is only a struggle we're having *in thought* — a fight against shadows and lies. Eddy tell us: "To strike out right and left against the mist, never clears the vision; but to lift your head above it, is a sovereign panacea."[36] We can strive fearlessly, when we know the outcome. We can boldly proclaim the supremacy of Good. Whatever we must face, we can wisely choose our five smooth stones. We won't lose, because God has already won.

A *test* or *trial* can also be a *temptation*. Many dictionary meanings for the words *tempt, trial,* and *test* are interchangeable — involving not only the dismissal of errors but also the resistance to seduction, and the refusal to take the bait or fall into any trap set by wrong thinking. When you are awake to the Truth, you won't be fooled by the decoy — you'll know immediately it's not the genuine article.

In the Lord's Prayer (Matthew 6:9–13; see The Law of Principle chapter), one line says: "and lead us not into temptation." Satan (evil, error) is also known as The Temptor and "the father of lies," so asking for strength to resist temptation is significant, since the next line of the prayer is "but deliver us from evil." The prayer is declaring here that evil is counterfeit, a lie, a trick — and certainly something from which God will always rescue us.

Since we're not yet at a point of complete enlightenment, how do we allay our sometimes overwhelming fears when we must face life's crises and uncertainties? Dr. Chopra suggests a rather remarkable prayer:

> The more uncertain things seem to be, the more secure I will
> feel, because uncertainty is my path to freedom.... I will step into
> the field of all possibilities and anticipate the excitement that
> can occur when I remain open to an infinity of choices.[37]

When yielding to "the wisdom of uncertainty," Chopra says that "the law of detachment" goes into effect.[38] I would add further that we are liberated from the fetters of matter to align with Mind. Thus apparent uncertainty can be our "path to freedom." This isn't giving up; it's getting in to real Life. When we know what Life really is, and who we really are, then we're not going to be fooled by a suppositional *rule* of uncertainty, which would proclaim that randomness is the *norm* and nothing can be counted on.

There has been put forth a "principle of uncertainty" in quantum physics, with which Albert Einstein vehemently disagreed: Einstein insisted that "God does not play dice."[39] Although Einstein's statement is disputed by many physicists today, my question is this: What if "uncertainty" is merely an indication of our ability to make choices — all of them right — as expressions of Infinite Mind, which is forever full of good ideas? We don't have to be tricked by a false picture of so-called chaos. We can choose the certainty of Principle. Without a trace of doubt, we can possess this great wisdom about what *appears* to be uncertainty. Our affirmation of the certainty of Truth will transform any difficult situation.

When I get into a state of self-criticism, denigrating myself for not having reached a certain point I'm supposedly to have arrived at by now in my life, after a while I eventually get to the realization that *I am always at a certain point*. Love, Truth, Life, All — in Spirit — *is* certain, steady, stable, and harmonious. This is the only "point" where any of us exists.

"Be of good cheer," advises Eddy: "the warfare with one's self is grand; it gives one plenty of employment, and the divine Principle worketh with you, — and obedience crowns persistent effort with everlasting victory."[40] Consequently the Apostle Paul seeming to gush over his own suffering — taking "pleasure in infirmities" — is not so perplexing, but makes perfect sense (see II Corinthians 12:7–10).

If each of us is to prove the Truth of Being in practical terms that we can apply each moment of every day, then we must be diligent about it — for ourselves and for each other. It's important to be vigilant, but never naive. Evil unchallenged is evil increased. We must be ever-alert. More than half the battle is about staying awake. "Stand porter at the door of thought," counsels Eddy. Allow in only those thoughts you want to be realized in bodily results, and you will control yourself harmoniously.[41] When challenged by any difficulty, physical or otherwise, we can hold to the fact that Good is the One and Only Power. Good is Life, Life is Spirit, and we are Spirit's expression, so the body is spiritual. Because Good is Infinite and Omnipotent, evil is impotent. Good has no evil side. Thus there is only one side to reality: the good side.[42]

> Are we willing to stop looking to the false view that we are living in matter, to stop looking for material solutions in times of trouble? Material choices always disappoint, they can never fully solve anything — so matter brings only more sorrow, decline, disarray, and ultimately death. When we're willing to give up the useless striving to hold onto matter (which, being unreal, is perpetually baffling, impossible to pin down), only *then* can

we get on to the real business of Life. Then we can prove our permanent connection with God.[43]

The following happened to me some years ago when the cash flow for my editing business wasn't going very well:

> One day I was agonizing over particular clients who hadn't paid their invoices on time, and there were significant bills we could not pay. I knew there was nothing to be done to force someone to pay us, yet I wondered how in the world we would make ends meet that week. In frustration, I went outside to take a walk so that I could think clearly enough to pray. It was still difficult. The mountainous landscape around my house is breathtaking, majestic, with a tranquillity that is exceptionally awe-inspiring. Yet, I was *not* inspired now. I trudged along with frustration, trying The Lord's Prayer, Mary Baker Eddy's Scientific Statement of Being, and The Prayer of St. Francis, but I couldn't even stick with more than one phrase without my thought wandering off once again to looking at how impossible it all was. I redoubled my efforts and turned to God wholeheartedly.
>
> Then, at the top of a hill, almost back home again, I looked down at the ground and saw a shiny round button in the street, the kind with a stickpin and a saying on it. The jazzy words jumped out at me: *Lighten up, none of this is real.*
>
> I laughed out loud, thankful that when we pray, the divine Truth of what *is* real gets through to us — whatever it takes!
>
> On a walk the very next day, that button was nowhere to be found. I checked the mailbox, and one of our clients had come through with a payment, while another major client paid unexpectedly early! Indeed, the only reality that whole time was the eternal supply of good — expressed through my work and the gratitude of others for it.

Pioneers Of Thought

> "Science says: All is Mind and Mind's idea. You must fight it out on this line. Matter can afford you no aid." — Mary Baker Eddy[44]

It's true that we can't demonstrate what we don't yet understand.[45] OK, so maybe you yourself haven't walked on water, raised someone from the dead, passed through a wall, defied the law of gravity (is it *really* an unbreakable "law"?), or learned to live without food or air — *yet*! However, there are documented cases of yogi masters and others who are able to materialize and dematerialize at will, levitate, and even live without eating. Giri Bala, the "Non-Eating Saint," is known to have lived for over fifty years without food or drink, and never got sick.[46] It is even possible to live without breathing: In 1947 Dr. Alvan L. Barach of the College of Physicians and Surgeons in New York originated a "lung-rest therapy" of "non-breathing" that lasted for hours; the treatments restored health to many tuberculosis sufferers, rested the body, heart, and mind, and even took away all desire for cigarettes for patients who had been heavy smokers.[47] Although ordinary people have to stay in an equalizing pressure chamber to obtain the benefits of non-breathing, the yogi achieves the same thing through spiritual understanding. Through spiritual advancement, a yogi "cognize[s] the breath as a mental concept, an act of mind: a dream breath.... [The yogi] scientifically makes breathing unnecessary, and does not enter (during the hours of practice) the negative states of sleep, unconsciousness, or death."[48] Just because we haven't achieved these things personally yet doesn't mean they aren't possible. With God, *anything is possible*. (Remember, Nothing is impossible!) When we awaken to this fact, our experience of reality becomes whatever we are ready and willing to accept into our thought.

Centuries ago people believed it was preposterous to think we could fly. But nowadays we have airplanes, even routine space travel. We have *always* possessed the ability to fly — we just had to discover it. We may think it's impossible for people to "beam" from one locale to another à là *Star Trek*; but why is that any more inconceivable than the invention of the fax, the magic of radio and television, the computer, the Internet, the cellphone, or a GPS device? It took "crazy" believers to demonstrate these marvels, and with conviction and determination they made them a part of our common experience. You and I, too, can be new pioneers of thought. Eddy encourages us, proclaiming: "The time for thinkers has come."[49] A woman of the late 19th century, she was just beginning to celebrate the many new inventions of the Industrial Age such as the telephone, wireless, electric light, and typewriter — and she could see these provided just a glimpse of the future. She cautions us not to judge future advancements by the steps already taken "lest you yourself be condemned for failing to take the first step."[50] Let's keep our hearts and minds open.

What Dreams May Come

"To sleep! perchance to dream; ay, there's the rub;

For in that sleep of death what dreams may come,

When we have shuffled off this mortal coil,

Must give us pause." — William Shakespeare, *Hamlet*

When we ascend into heaven, or descend into hell, these are not localities, but modes of thought. Our state of mind, moment by moment, dictates whether we're in heaven or in hell. Are we listening to evil or to Good? Are we choosing to follow a path that leads to death or to Life? The choices are always up to each of us. We are subject only to Divine Law; we can either defend our rights (and our neighbors') under this Law as God's children, and seek spiritual solutions and regeneration — or we can ignore our divine childhood and look the other way, back into matter, seeking comfort and assistance from material things.

In the fascinating 1998 film *What Dreams May Come* (directed by Vincent Ward and based on the novel by Richard Matheson) the main character Chris (played by Robin Williams) is killed in a car accident, only to find out that his life's journey has just begun in a heaven of his own making. He begins to discover that whatever he wants to experience he can bring about by tapping into his imagination — sparked by the world of his beloved wife Annie's paintings. When Annie (Annabella Sciorra) later kills herself in grief, she is condemned to hell — a realm of her own making. Chris' afterlife guide, Albert (Cuba Gooding Jr.), explains that suicides confine themselves to a darkness of despair that can never be broken. Chris refuses to accept this, and decides to go into hell itself to find her, armed only with his stubborn determination and unconditional love.

As he descends into perdition Chris comes upon countless sufferers locked into a never-ending cycle of agony. The most effective picture of this nightmare to me is a sea of heads — like steppingstones over which Chris must walk — each twisted face reciting a torrent of mundane, everyday complaints.

Annie's personal hell is a dark and crumbling version of their home, filled with haunting memories of her dead husband and children (their son and daughter also died in a car accident). Because Annie has locked herself into this world of hopelessness, she doesn't recognize Chris and is even fearful and hostile toward him. Nevertheless, Chris is so full of compassion he decides to stay with her in hell anyway. Once he makes this decision, it isn't long before she suddenly awakens to the reality of his love, making it possible for them to return to paradise together, and to a new beginning.

To me this story not only illustrates everlasting Life, it is also a metaphor for the way Love works: God always loves unconditionally, no matter what. The I AM THAT I AM can't do otherwise. Even when we're in the pit of despair, God stays with us. Whenever we choose to listen to the truth of Love, we enter a heaven of new hope and new possibilities. Life welcomes us to a place of reassurance, safety, transformation, and healing.

When Jesus said "Repent, for the kingdom of heaven is at hand" (see Matthew 4:17), he was telling us: "Think again! Turn around! Look again! The reign of perfection is right here."

Advancing Years

"Do not go gentle into that good night,

Old age should burn and rave at close of day;

Rage, rage against the dying of the light." — Dylan Thomas[51]

Albert Einstein once wrote in a letter to a friend discussing the subject of death: "the past, present and future are only illusions, however persistent." According to Einstein's Theory of Relativity, time does not "happen" bit by bit: it is stretched out, as space is, in its entirety.[52]

Nevertheless, in common thinking, we all buy into the pervasive lie of birth, decline, and death. The path to breaking ourselves of this habit must be in awakening — an awareness of Life as It truly is: Spirit, not matter. We can start by looking at how often we refer to age — and right here and now we can decide to stop the relentless noting and recording of ages.[53] We can help our children do this too, by avoiding (or at least deemphasizing) the significance of birthdays: We can choose to honor Life each day. Like the Mad Hatter in *Alice in Wonderland*, we can happily celebrate all our "unbirthdays."

We can at least begin to watch and modify the words we use. Think about it. Here's one example: We can't "grow old" — it's impossible! — we can only "grow new"! The fact is, we can never regress. We cannot diminish or degenerate, since we are spiritual ideas, not physical entities. We can only be *advancing,* never declining. This fact redeems the phrase "advancing years."

So what difference does it make "how old" we are? Age is an *artificial concept* that comes from measuring how many times our planet revolves around our sun. Then we decide to connect this number with our identity. But this measurement is an irrelevant exercise. God doesn't revolve around something and then desire to measure it. Being Infinite — Infinite Being — Life can't be measured. Life just *is*. Each of us is Life's offspring — thus reflecting limitless Life. What if we really took this truth to heart?

We all know people who seem younger than their years without plastic surgery or make-up — because of the way they live (i.e., the way they think). Our attitudes literally shape who we are. Mary Baker Eddy tells the true story, cited from the London medical journal *The Lancet*, in which a woman does not age:

> Disappointed in love in her early years, she became insane and lost all account of time. Believing that she was still living in the same hour which parted her from her lover, taking no note of years, she stood daily before the window watching for her lover's coming. In this mental state she remained young. Having no consciousness of time, she literally grew no older. Some American travellers saw her when she was seventy-four, and supposed her to be a young woman. She had no care-lined face, no wrinkles nor gray hair, but youth sat gently on cheek and brow. Asked to guess her age, those unacquainted with her history conjectured that she must be under twenty.
>
> This instance of youth preserved furnishes a useful hint, upon which a Franklin might work with more certainty than when he coaxed the enamoured lightning from the clouds. Years had not made her old, because she had taken no cognizance of passing time nor thought of herself as growing old. The bodily results of her belief that she was young manifested the influence of such a belief. She could not age while believing herself young, for the mental state governed the physical.
>
> Impossibilities never occur. One instance like the foregoing proves it possible to be young at seventy-four; and the primary of that illustration makes it plain that decrepitude is not according to law, nor is it a necessity of nature, but an illusion.[54]

The human aging process is but a belief in the passing of time, the belief that growth, decline, and death are predictable and inevitable because of the Earth revolving around the sun. But when we know that even what we perceive as this "moment" or the "now" is simply *awareness* — without "past," "present," or "future" — we can choose, with each and every thought, what we will accept as true about our identity and potential. Dr. Chopra describes the aging process as simply a manifestation of how we perceive the passage of time, the ways we experience change. For instance, if we always feel we're lacking enough time, struggling to beat deadlines, etc., the hormone levels stay up, blood pressure is higher, and the heart beats faster; on the other hand, when we're relaxed, feeling like we have all the time in the world, the body's rhythms are slower. These perceptions affect all our experiences and therefore our overall well-being and life-span.[55]

When death does occur, it is only a transition from one state of consciousness to another based upon our level of understanding of what's spiritually true. Someone may seem to leave our sight (or when we die we may seem to leave), but this experience happens only because we are limiting our own ways of seeing. Life is eternal. Our loved ones' lives continue to progress, even if unseen to human eyes.[56] A person who dies is simply beyond the extent of our awareness, like a ship sailing over the horizon, or a seagull flying off into the distance.[57]

Consciousness Constructs The Body

"Let us therefore, as many as be perfect, be thus minded: and if in any thing ye be otherwise minded, God shall reveal even this unto you." (Philippians 3:15)

Wherever we are mentally is what we experience physically. Once we get in the habit of acknowledging our identity as spiritual rather than material, our experience of wellness and fitness shifts. Consciousness constructs a better body whenever faith in matter is conquered.[58] With an understanding of Life as Spirit, we are able to discern where the errors are in our thinking. Most often they've sneaked in without us realizing it. As our awareness increases, the false beliefs (e.g., bad habits) eventually will become so obvious, we will see each set of circumstances in a new light. We'll then see *the spiritual reality* rather than the material picture — and heal the situation. Then Life makes a lot more sense: It's very clear what to do when we realize that all experience takes place in a mental rather than in a physical realm.

For example, from a *spiritual perspective*, losing weight is about dedicating ourselves in a whole new way to eating right (expressing balance, beauty, and joy through cooking and eating), and to exercising (expressing mastery, grace, and love through all of our actions). And it's so much more. It's about *losing* whatever negativity is *weighing* us down. It's practicing how to *throw our weight* on the right side of any challenge (the spiritual side). As we learn from this process, we can begin to recognize that we don't have to *wait* for Good to happen. We can claim it every moment by acknowledging that our *life is God*. That means our nourishment is spiritual — it originates in Infinite Life Itself. True sustenance comes from peace, patience, and an understanding of Divine lovingkindness.[59] When we reclaim every quality of Life as spiritual rather than material, the body adjusts and maintains its proper weight and fitness.

All bodily functions are governed and expressed by Mind, and thus harmonious. Consequently there is One Power governing all action.

The acceptance of this fact healed a severe case of food poisoning instantaneously when a friend of mine realized that some fish she ate could not wield a power over her greater than God. I once put my hand on my husband's feverish forehead, absolutely certain that no belief of a so-called power outside of God called "fever" could afflict him; his skin was suddenly cool to the touch. I have burned my hand while cooking, immediately declared in my thought that a spiritual being cannot be harmed, and after only passing pain, have had no injury.

The next time you stub your toe on the furniture and feel the excruciating pain, instead of resigning yourself to it, directly proclaim "I am not material, I am spiritual" (out loud if you have to)! With practice, as your spiritual understanding increases, in each instance the pain will dissipate a lot faster. After all, how can the good idea of a sofa (the manifestation of comfort, relaxation, and home) harm a complete idea of God? Feeling no pain at all *is* ultimately possible.

I recently cut my finger with a sharp knife while chopping vegetables, and I felt no pain even though bleeding was profuse. The next day I played guitar for an audience and did not need a Band-Aid, nor did I feel any discomfort. I had forgotten all about it. Someone I know accidentally hit her thumb so hard that the thumbnail came off, yet she felt no pain in the least. She explains that she vehemently maintained at the time that her thought was more powerful than what appeared to have taken place physically. Mary Baker Eddy says: "When an accident happens, you think or exclaim, 'I am hurt!' Your thought is more powerful than your words, more powerful than the accident itself, to make the injury real."[60] A friend of mine who accidentally hit his thumb with a hammer decided to declare immediately that he wasn't hurt — because he acknowledged the fact that a material dream cannot hurt, and that there isn't any pain in Spirit. As he watched his thumb turn colors, he quickly chose to turn away and decided not to look at the thumb while he continued to affirm that he wasn't hurt. Several hours later the injury had disappeared.

There are documented cases of multiple personality disorder in which an individual has a chronic illness while displaying one personality, yet shows no symptoms whatsoever of that disease while expressing another personality. These people can often switch personalities instantly, going from diabetic to normal; from drunk to sober; from an allergic rash to completely clear skin; from a need for glasses to 20/20 vision; even disfiguring scars can disappear and reappear; one personality can be anesthetized during surgery while another suddenly wakes up.[61] These examples are signs to us of what is indeed possible. Our opportunities for spiritual growth are endless.

According to Bernie Siegel, MD, author of the best-seller *Love, Medicine, and Miracles*, patients often describe their experiences with ailments as spiritual or emotional challenges — such as a mastectomy patient who felt she needed "to get something off her chest," or the man with carcinoma of the larynx whose father had punished him as a child by constantly squeezing his throat.[62] How typical it is to have an aching back when feeling weighed down by a problem, or when criticized by higher-ups (wishing they'd get "off our back"). Whatever we entertain in thought is manifested in our experience — perhaps not as dramatically as in the 1956 sci-fi classic film *Forbidden Planet,* but certainly more than most of us realize. Nevertheless, this is *not* to say that we *deserve* illness or suffering, nor that contracting a disease or enduring misfortune is our fault. On the contrary, when the spiritual reality is recognized and the material picture is viewed as *only mental,* we can see we are not guilty of anything because God made us blameless and pure. The Apostle Paul said there is no condemnation for people who live in the Spirit instead of the flesh. Paul also wrote that the Law of Spirit cancels out the so-called law that says sin and death are inevitable (see Romans 8:1–2). We can throw the erroneous thoughts away. If there is sin to be corrected, we will recognize that too, and send it packing. This prayerful process doesn't take willpower, but insight: The moment of understanding is the healing.

Spiritual awareness gives new meaning to so-called psychosomatic illness. Webster's says that *psychosomatic* means "relating to, involving, or concerned with bodily symptoms caused by mental or emotional disturbance," yet often these ailments are discounted as somehow imaginary, while other supposed organic or systemic diseases are deemed serious. Scientific prayer works in every case, when we know that *all* discord — physical, environmental, financial, emotional, etc. — is caused by "mental disturbance." No matter how foolish or dire a problem may appear, it will vanish once we align our thought back to God's. Remember, prayer is not an attempt to reprogram a material human mind; instead we're acknowledging our intact identity as a Divine idea within the One Mind.[63]

Life's same Principle applies, eradicating every mistake when it comes to human beliefs about so-called laws of heredity, DNA, family history, birth order, astrological signs, nutrition, blood pressure, cholesterol, etc. Any expectations we hold regarding current medical theories, prognoses based on statistics, destiny based on the stars, or a fate preordained by our circumstances will certainly have an effect on how we conduct our behavior and how we live our lives. But since we exist in God's care, we are never condemned to any particular set of events. Instead of resigning ourselves to the dire predictions we hear from society and in the media — particularly in advertisements that tell us we are needy and unwell, constantly pitching to us the idea that we can't survive without continuous remedies — we can choose the spiritual reality and rise above the lie of so-called physical conditions.

It's heartening to note that some scientists actually do recognize the counterfeit nature of disease. For instance, it has been found that a virus "does not even satisfy one of the criteria for life [the capacity to reproduce, respond to stimuli, grow, etc.].... A virus can multiply only by invading a host cell and taking over its biochemical functions.... It could be argued that under these circumstances the *cell* is no longer living, since it has lost the ability to reproduce *itself*."[64] In light of this fact, the question becomes: Shall we give credence to a virus's supposed power to make a person ill? Shall we choose to "catch a bug"? Or shall we step out of the pitcher's line of sight? A virus is an unwelcome visitor in our thinking that need not be entertained. The only way sickness can take hold is when we invite it in, give it guest towels, fluff the pillows, and ask it to make itself at home! If we slam the door shut instead, the belief is gone and thus the symptoms disappear. I am certain that some day in the future it will be discovered by the scientific establishment that diseased cells in the body are literally the *result* of mistaken thinking, rather than the actual *cause* of physical discord. In the meantime, we can prove it for ourselves in living out healthier lives.

Perfect Parenting

"Don't we all have One Father-Mother God? Hasn't One God created us?" — (see Malachi 2:10)

One of the greatest gifts we can give our children is an understanding of scientific prayer. Children are so open to the Truth, so willing to listen to Spirit. We can model for them the habit of turning to our Father-Mother God as a first resort for help, and then watch all the countless healings take place. Mary Baker Eddy's words of advice ring true:

Mind regulates the condition of the stomach, bowels, and food, the temperature of children and of men, and matter does not. The wise or unwise views of parents and other persons on these subjects produce good or bad effects on the health of children....

Giving drugs to infants, noticing every symptom of flatulency, and constantly directing the mind to such signs — that mind being laden with illusions about disease, health-laws, and death — these actions convey mental images to children's budding thoughts, and often stamp them there, making it probable at any time that such ills may be reproduced in the very ailments feared. A child may have worms, if you say so, or any other malady, timorously held in the beliefs concerning his body. Thus are laid the foundations of the belief in disease and death, and thus are children educated into discord.[65]

The entire education of children should be such as to form habits of obedience to the moral and spiritual law, with which the child can meet and master the belief in so-called physical laws, a belief which breeds disease.

If parents create in their babes a desire for incessant amusement, to be always fed, rocked, tossed, or talked to, those parents should not, in after years, complain of their children's fretfulness or frivolity, which the parents themselves have occasioned. Taking less "thought for your life, what ye shall eat, or what ye shall drink"; less thought "for your body what ye shall put on," [see Matthew 6:25–26] will do much more for the health of the rising generation than you dream.[66]

Hitting that mute button whenever the TV commercials come on (especially those regarding ailments or drugs), becomes much more important when we realize how vital it is to defend our own well-being. Conversation about "colds going around"; listening to idle chatter about "allergy season" or "flu season"; taking in tales from friends and strangers about the symptoms of diseases — all can literally be harmful to our health. It is essential that we guard our own thought against the suppositions of world opinion as much as possible, and teach our children to do so as well. I guarantee: If you insist on choosing the spiritual reality, and make this prayerful process a part of your daily routine, then your health — and your family's as well — will markedly improve.

Parenting is so much easier when we utilize the tools of scientific prayer. Eddy relates:

A little girl, who had occasionally listened to my explanations, badly wounded her finger. She seemed not to notice it. On being questioned about it she answered ingenuously, "There is no sensation in matter." Bounding off with laughing eyes, she presently added, "Mamma, my finger is not a bit sore."
....Children should be taught the Truth-cure, Christian Science, among their first lessons, and kept from discussing or

entertaining theories or thoughts about sickness. To prevent the experience of error and its sufferings, keep out of the minds of your children either sinful or diseased thoughts.[67]

If a child is exposed to contagion or infection, the mother is frightened and says, "My child will be sick." The law of mortal mind and her own fears govern her child more than the child's mind governs itself, and they produce the very results which might have been prevented through the opposite understanding.

Then it is believed that exposure to the contagion wrought the mischief. That mother...need[s] better guidance, who says to her child: "You look sick," "You look tired," "You need rest," or "You need medicine."

Such a mother runs to her little one, who thinks she has hurt her face by falling on the carpet, and says, moaning more childishly than her child, "Mamma knows you are hurt." The better and more successful method for any mother to adopt is to say: "Oh, never mind! You're not hurt, so don't think you are." Presently the child forgets all about the accident, and is at play.[68]

Here is an incident from my own life:

When my daughter was two years old, one day at lunch she refused to eat. We got into a shouting match. To catch my breath, I went to pick up a glass of water — and it broke in my hand.

Blood was pouring all over, and now we were *both* crying. As I held my hand under the faucet, I finally woke up. I took a deep breath, sat down with a wet towel in my hand, got the shards out as best I could, and phoned my husband to tell him what had happened. Through all of this, our daughter was still bawling! I asked him for help: Could he talk to her on the phone and get her to be quiet?

She took the phone and I turned to God for guidance: "How can I do this better?" I prayed, sorry for all my yelling. Then, as I forgave myself for not being a perfect parent, it came to me very clearly that I could let myself off the hook: I decided to allow my daughter to choose whether or not she would eat.

Soon the blood slowed, and there was no more glass in the hand. That minute, my daughter started singing sweetly part of a prayer she knew [written by Mary Baker Eddy — see the *Children's Prayer* at the end of the chapter on the Law of Principle], applying it to *me*: "Father-Mother God, loving Mommy, guide her little feet up to Thee."

I welled up with gratitude for God, the One loving Parent that was protecting all three of us. I found myself smiling — almost laughing — with joy. In that instant I knew I was fine. I felt peaceful, probably for the first time that day. The bleeding stopped, my daughter ate without a fuss, and I was able to clean up the mess without incident.

Although the cut had looked severe, two days later there was almost no sign of it whatsoever. I was also thankful for the lesson which has stayed with me: In any challenge, a moment of quiet to turn to God is all the resolve I need.[69]

The knowledge that our Father-Mother God is always parenting us — both grown-ups and children — frees us to unshoulder the burden of false responsibility. Here is another case in point from a woman who challenged this burden. Her story:

She and her husband had an argument after she tried to wake him up. Once in a while this would happen without explanation, and each time she would get very upset when he lashed out at her about trying to awaken him. He often worked during the night and woke up in the afternoon — whereas she was usually up in the morning.

When he was a child, he was a very heavy sleeper, and his mother used to yell in his ear to startle him, or she'd kick him to wake him up. This really traumatized him as a kid. Now, sometimes when he was still groggy, if he heard his wife saying something sweetly such as, "time to wake up," in his drowsy state he would think instead that his mother was yelling at him. He didn't hear his wife actually saying something in a soothing voice. Suddenly he would be very upset, and tell her she was treating him terribly; he would quote things she never said, because he was dreaming that she said them.

Needless to say, whenever this happened it was extremely disconcerting, and the wife felt helpless to defend herself. She felt like there was nothing she could do to convince him that she wasn't saying cruel things to him, when he was convinced in his half-awake state that she said them.

This time, as he stomped off angrily into the shower, she stewed self-righteously, feeling more and more furious at his mother for traumatizing him so. Her thoughts were churning, as she rehearsed a big speech to him that went something like: "Guess what. I am *not* your mother and *nothing like your mother*, and you have *no right* to put me into that role, or tell me that I am in any way treating you in the terrible way your mother once did...."

Then, as she wiped away tears, she realized she didn't want to fight, she wanted to pray. She quieted down her raging thoughts and asked for Divine guidance. "What else can I do in this situation?" she pleaded.

In less than a minute, the message came like a thunderbolt: *God is the only Mother.* Just like that — she wasn't angry any more! She told herself, "It's true, you are not his mother; he has only One Mother, and She would never mistreat Her son! So you don't have to be angry at anyone!"

Right then and there, she happily thanked God for the answer she needed. She decided to drop the whole thing and not say another word about it. And when her husband got out of the shower, instead of still harboring anger, he had also put it all aside, and they spent a pleasant day together, as if it had never happened.

The powerful message that *God is the only Parent* helps so often to diffuse a situation whenever I myself am challenged by my own role of motherhood. The qualities of our One Father-Mother God are forever alive in each of us; everything Good already exists within ourselves.[70] As we face the formidable task of parenthood with a prayerful attitude, claiming our own divine childhood while acknowledging every step of the way that the pure Goodness of Life is the ruling authority for everyone, right guidance from God will always come. Then we can accept this important responsibility joyfully — knowing that our "response-ability," which springs from Life, makes us ever "able to respond" with wisdom.

"What Is The Matrix?"

"Propel, propel, propel your craft

Gently down liquid solution

Ecstatically, ecstatically, ecstatically, ecstatically,

Existence is but an illusion."

— Fred Rogers' version of *Row, Row, Row Your Boat,* singing as King Friday the XIIIth on the PBS-TV program *Mr. Rogers' Neighborhood*

The Matrix, the 1999 cyberthriller directed and written by Andy and Larry Wachowski, is worth discussing here because of the sheer magnitude of its implications. The premise of the story, which takes place in the not-so-distant future, is that what we think of as reality is instead a computer-generated dreamworld called The Matrix, created by machines of artificial intelligence to control all mankind. When the hero, Neo ("new" in Greek) (played by Keanu Reeves), encounters Morpheus[71] (Laurence Fishburne), the leader of a burgeoning underground revolt, Neo asks "What is The Matrix?" and is told the horrifying truth. Once Neo is acclimated to the devastating "real world," where all life as we know it was destroyed some time in the 21st century, Morpheus begins teaching him the rebels' strategy for battling The Matrix.

"As long as The Matrix exists, the human race will never be free," Morpheus tells him. He explains that most people are totally unaware that they are living in a mental projection, controlled by the same rules as a computer program. In other words, all the laws work (e.g., gravity), because they are part of the program. "Your mind makes it real," says Morpheus. If you're killed in The Matrix, you die in The Matrix, because you believe your body exists there. "The body cannot live without the mind," Morpheus explains.

Morpheus connects them to virtual-reality scenarios inside computer programs, where he teaches Neo the art of kung fu, and Neo begins to learn that anything is possible. Morpheus points out: "Do you believe that my being stronger or faster has anything to do with my muscles in this place? You think that's *air* you're breathing now?" He tells Neo: "You're faster than this. Don't think you are. *Know* you are." Morpheus reveals the goal of all this training: "I'm trying to free your mind, Neo. But I can only show you the door. You're the one who has to walk through it." As Neo's understanding and skills grow, Neo becomes able to enter other computer programs where he can run faster than anyone else, jump from building to building, and even jump off skyscrapers and land without a scratch.

In one scene Neo sees children who can make building blocks fly, and observes one child who can bend a spoon just by looking at it. The child says to him, "Do not try and bend the spoon. That's impossible. Instead, only try to realize the truth." "What truth?" Neo wonders. "There is no spoon," the child replies. "Then you'll see that it is not the spoon that bends, it is only yourself." At this point Neo bends a spoon in the same way.

The reason Neo soon learns to defy the rules of The Matrix is because he is *awake* to reality. Neo is one of the few people who knows that the "rules" controlling The Matrix can be broken. In the end he is even able to dodge a barrage of bullets from the enemy agents.

The Matrix is a fable worth retelling, because it is such a powerful illustration of the myth of matter vs. the reality of Life. As we prayerfully follow a spiritual path, we can learn many lessons from this film. We may not yet personally be leaping off tall buildings without injury or avoiding bullets, yet we know these feats are *not* out of the realm of possibility.[72]

Nigel Hutchinson-Brooks, a parachutist in military training, jumped from an airplane with his fellow soldiers only to be buffeted by a gust of wind into another man's parachute. "As his parachute opened, I fell feet first right between his rigging lines and out the other side. My parachute never opened; it just bunched into a great glob of canvas and slid down the rigging lines, completely covering his head, face, and shoulders, and collapsing his parachute." This happened when they were only 800 feet from the ground. They were falling a lot faster than normal. "Below, I saw a khaki vehicle with a big red cross on its roof racing toward where we were headed. 'Uh-oh,' I thought to myself, 'they think we're in trouble!'"

As it so happened, in the few weeks before that particular exercise Hutchinson-Brooks had been studying the 91st Psalm, especially the first verse: "He that dwelleth in the secret place of the most High shall abide under the shadow of the Almighty." He describes what happened next: "There was no time to think the words — the concepts just came straight to my mind."

He thought, "All right, God, it's up to You, because there's nothing I can do." He later heard from the people watching on the ground that he hit the ground, rolled, bounced ten feet into the air, and landed, sprawled out. Yet right away he was up on his feet. "And the other man was OK, too. We both got up and walked away." Hutchinson-Brooks provides this explanation of what happened: "In a situation in which the laws of physics dictate that the human body can handle only a certain level of force, God revealed those so-called laws to be null and void.... We'd hit the ground at almost seventy miles an hour. The ambulance crew just shook their heads in disbelief.... If you obey the laws of God and are conscious that [God] is your helper, your protector, and the source of your being it's amazing what will happen."[73]

It's barely beginning to dawn on us as a species that matter isn't real. But once we know something, we can't *un*know it. We can only continue to demonstrate Truth, proving it for ourselves and sharing it with others as best we can. Even as we make our small experimental steps into this amazing new reality, this awkward journey is still a vast improvement over the outgrown and deeply dissatisfying myth that defined us as carbon-based mechanisms trapped in a material world.

This new understanding of Life will, at the very least, make us healthier, elevate our character, and increase our longevity, as we see that we can exceed ordinary human capabilities.[74] Recognition of the spiritual determines the outward and actual.[75] As pioneers of thought we will transform the universe. Let the following prayer from The Upanishads be our refrain:

Lead me from the unreal to the Real.
Lead me from darkness to Light.
Lead me from death to Immortality.[76]

LIFE

being

verve

vital force

creature

animation

SPIRIT

brio

élan

vigor

perennial

existence

PRINCIPLE

activity

experience

resilience

quickening

enlivened

effervescence

flavor

essence

oomph

dash

SOUL

vim

zing

continuing

enduring

growth

idea

effectiveness

liveliness

elasticity

vivified

precious

sparkle

fresh

nature

consciousness

sharp

inception

continuous cycle

birth

supplies

duration

complete

confidence

momentum

unbroken

cause

action

sum and substance

development

lasting

preservation

task

assurance

source

connected

whole

origin

good humor

biography

memoir

basic nature

esprit

THESE BLANK PAGES FOR YOUR NOTES AND PRAYERS

ENDNOTES

THE LAW OF LIFE CONQUERS DEATH

1 Quoted in *S&H*, p. 104:8–12.

2 *The Planetary Mind* by Arne A. Wyller. Aspen, CO: MacMurray & Beck, 1996, p. 1. Hereinafter referred to as *Planetary Mind*.

3 *Planetary Mind*, p. 143–144.

4 See *Planetary Mind*, p. 168, 170, 172.

5 *Spiritual Evolution*, p. 53.

6 *Spiritual Evolution*, p. 130.

7 *Spiritual Evolution*, p. 134.

8 *Matter Myth*, p. 260.

9 See *Planetary Mind*, p. 229.

10 See *Planetary Mind*, p. 218.

11 See *Holographic Universe*, p. 33, 50.

12 See *Planetary Mind*, p. 172.

13 *Miscellaneous Writings*, p. 190:1–10.

14 From *Fulfilling Your Spiritual Promise* by John-Roger. Los Angeles: Mandeville Press, 2006. John-Roger is the founder of the Movement of Spiritual Inner Awareness (MSIA) and also the author of *Spiritual Warrior: The Art of Spiritual Living*.

15 The Apostle Paul also mentions this in Ephesians 5:8 and in I Thessalonians 5:5.

16 *Autobiography of a Yogi*, by Paramahansa Yogananda. Los Angeles: Self-Realization Fellowship, 1946 (13th ed. ©1998), p. 315, 316. Italics are in the original. Hereinafter referred to as *Autobiography of a Yogi*.

17 *The Age of Spiritual Machines: When Computers Exceed Human Intelligence* by Ray Kurzweil. New York: Viking, 1999, p. 280. Hereinafter referred to as *Age of Spiritual Machines*.

18   *Holographic Universe,* p. 26.

19   From Rupert Sheldrake's interview in 1987 on the TV program
Thinking Allowed, "New Physics and Beyond" (this segment, #Q124, is a
four-episode video which contains an interview of Sheldrake as well as
of Fred Alan Wolf, Saul-Paul Sirag, and Nick Herbert). A weekly public
television series hosted by Jeffrey Mishlove — celebrated author of
The Roots of Consciousness, with a doctorate in parapsychology from the
University of California at Berkeley — *Thinking Allowed* features interviews
with physicists, scientists and other leading thinkers. Available on video
from Thinking Allowed Productions, 2560 Ninth Street, Ste. 123, Berkeley,
CA 94710, tel. 510/548-4415 or 800/999-4415. Transcripts also available.
Hereinafter referred to as *Thinking Allowed.*

   For more on Sheldrake's research, read his book, *Dogs That Know When
Their Owners Are Coming Home and Other Unexplained Powers of Animals.* New
York: Three Rivers Press, 1999.

20   From *Age of Spiritual Machines,* p. 78–79.

21   *Holographic Universe,* p. 137.

22   *Holographic Universe,* p. 219.

23   See *Holographic Universe,* p. 89.

24   See *S&H,* p. 547:25–27.

25   "Infinity and Individuality." See also *S&H,* p. 123:12 and p. 269:11.

26   "Would it be All Right With You if Life Got Easier?" Maria Nemeth
interview with Michael Toms, *New Dimensions* radio program, July 15, 2002.
Maria Nemeth has written *The Energy of Money: A Spiritual Guide to Financial
and Spiritual Fulfillment.* She gives workshops on "Mastering Life's Energies"
and runs The Academy for Coaching Excellence.

27   *The Four Agreements: A Practical Guide to Personal Freedom* by Don Miguel
Ruiz. San Rafael, CA: Amber-Allen Publishing, 1997, p. 16. Ruiz, who
conducts workshops around the world on the Toltec mystery school
tradition, was a surgeon until he had a near-death experience, pulling his
two friends to safety after a car accident; he then returned to the study of
the ancient Mexican wisdom of his mother, a *curandera* (healer), and of his
grandfather, a *nagual* (shaman). Ruiz eventually became a *nagual* himself.

28   See *S&H* p. 44:5–45:31; p. 160:30–161:10 and p. 198:29–199:24, as

well as *Christian Healing: A Sermon Delivered at Boston,* by Mary Baker Eddy. Boston: The Christian Science Publishing Society, 1886, especially p. 6:26–10:12. Hereinafter referred to as *Christian Healing.*

29 See *S&H* p. xi:9–15.

30 *Holographic Universe,* p. 146–147.

31 See *S&H,* p. 451:2–4. Eddy is citing the Apostle Paul in II Corinthians 6:17.

32 For more testimonies of healing from people of all walks of life and many different religious traditions, read *When Prayers Are Answered: True Stories of Miraculous Healings Through Prayer,* by John Holmstrom. New York: The Berkley Publishing Group, 1995.

33 See *Miscellaneous Writings,* p. 10:12–22.

34 *Seven Spiritual Laws of Success,* p. 89.

35 *S&H,* p. 66:10–11.

36 *Miscellaneous Writings,* p. 355:16–18.

37 *Seven Spiritual Laws of Success,* p. 91–92.

38 *Seven Spiritual Laws of Success,* p. 81.

39 *Search for Superstrings,* p. 40.

40 *Miscellaneous Writings,* p. 118:24–28.

41 *S&H,* p. 392:24. See p. 391:29–393:3 for the full discussion of what it means to "stand porter at the door of thought."

42 See *Christian Healing,* p. 10:8–12.

43 "Is it Possible to Pray Without Ceasing?" by Harriet Berg Harvey, *The Christian Science Sentinel,* September 24, 1995, v. 97, no. 36, p. 20–23.

44 *S&H,* p. 492:19.

45 See *S&H,* p. 254:16–19.

46 Read the chapter entitled "The Woman Yogi Who Never Eats" in *Autobiography of a Yogi,* p. 525–538.

47 See *Autobiography of a Yogi*, p. 285.

48 *Autobiography of a Yogi*, p. 280–281.

49 *S&H*, p. vii:13.

50 *S&H*, p. 459:8–11.

51 Lines from "Do Not Go Gentle Into That Good Night," in *The Collected Poems of Dylan Thomas 1934–1952.* New York: New Directions Publishing, 1971, p. 128.

52 See *Matter Myth*, p. 82.

53 See *S&H*, p. 246:17. A friend of mine calls reading p. 244:23–250:32 "getting a beauty treatment."

54 *S&H*, p. 245:5–31.

55 See *Magical Mind, Magical Body.*

56 "A Year After Columbine," *The Christian Science Monitor*, April 20, 2000, p. 23. [No author's name given]

57 These metaphors are taken from the verse "Gone From My Sight" by Henry Scott Holland (from *Death is Nothing at All*, New York: Avon, 1989), and from a pamphlet entitled "The Passing of the Sea Gull," reprinted from *The Christian Science Monitor*, Boston: The Christian Science Publishing Society, 1927.

58 See *S&H*, p. 425:23–24.

59 See *S&H*, p. 365:31 and p. 388:12–30.

60 See *S&H* p. 397:8–22 for the full passage on how to handle accidents through prayer.

61 See *Holographic Universe*, p. 97–100. See also "Rethinking the Nature and Care of the Human Body" by Patricia Tupper Hyatt. *The Christian Science Journal,* v. 118, no. 1, January 2000, p. 20 (Hereinafter referred to as "Rethinking the Nature and Care of the Human Body").

62 *Holographic Universe*, p. 86. See also Bernie Siegel's book, *Love, Medicine, and Miracles*, New York: Harper & Row, 1986.

63 See "Rethinking the Nature and Care of the Human Body," p. 20–22.

64 *Matter Myth*, p. 286–287. Italics are in the original.

65 *S&H*, p. 413:7; 24.

66 *S&H*, p. 62:4–16.

67 *S&H* p. 237:1; 15–20.

68 *S&H*, p. 154:16–155:2.

69 This account was published in a longer version as an article for www. spirituality.com: "Resolved: Take a Moment for Prayer," by Janis Hunt Johnson, January 2002.

70 This sentence is actually my paraphrase of a toast made in honor of the character Jack's (Sean Hayes) father who just passed away, given by the character Nathan (Woody Harrelson) on an episode of the TV sitcom "Will and Grace," a season finale which first aired on May 17, 2001.

71 In Classical mythology, Morpheus was the god of dreams; the Greek root *morph* means "form" — and it's where the cinematography term *morph* originates, meaning computer-controlled special effects applied to change the appearance of forms.

72 I've quoted all dialog directly from *The Matrix*. Burbank, CA: Warner Bros., 1999. Additional facts on this film were taken from the DVD packaging, Burbank: Warner Home Video, 1999. For further information on *The Matrix* and its sequels visit: www.whatisthematrix.com.

73 "Jumpers Safe After Parachuting Accident," by Nigel Hutchinson-Brooks. *The Christian Science Sentinel,* v. 100, no. 27, July 6, 1998.

74 See *S&H,* p. 492:7–21 and p. 128:4–19.

75 See *S&H*, p. 254:20–23.

76 *Commentaries on the Vedas*, p. 55.

5

Capstone:
the final crowning point; finishing touch.

LOVE

Let's get radical.

"For I am persuaded,
that neither death, nor life,
nor angels, nor principalities,
nor powers, nor things present,
nor things to come,
nor height, nor depth,
nor any other creature,
shall be able to
separate us
from the love of God"
— Romans 8:38–39

THE LAW OF LOVE ELIMINATES FEAR

Love Abides

God is Love. No matter how hatred tries to rear its ugly head to destroy, Love abides: proclaiming Itself, inviting everyone to participate — to love and be loved unconditionally. Love calls us to be enveloped in absolute safety, to rely on Love's promise regardless of our circumstances. The Love I'm talking about is pure — *agape* (Greek) or *prema* (Sanskrit) — this Divine Love is permanent, unconditional, unmoving, eternal, without need, without expectation, without attachment, without desire. The Apostle Paul wrote these timeless words to the early Christians in Corinth: "Love is patient and kind; it is not jealous or boastful; it does not behave itself unseemly. Love does not insist on its own way; it is not irritable or resentful; it thinks no evil; it does not rejoice in iniquity, but rejoices in the truth. Love bears all things, believes all things, hopes all things, endures all things. Love never fails.... So faith, hope, love abide, these three; but the greatest of these is love" (see I Corinthians 13:4–8, 13). Let's explore how we might make Love real in our daily lives — really know Love, feel Love, understand Love, fully express Love.

Fear — Not!

"There is no fear in love; but perfect love casts out fear"
— I John 4:18

Why do we find it so hard to believe in and accept perfect Love, which is given so freely? Because we're too busy being afraid. When we're looking at life from a material basis, it seems extremely improbable that unconditional Love would have anything to do with us. If we assume we exist in a material world — just dealing with what we know with the five senses — then pretty much about everything around us instills fear. *Fear,* meaning "agitation," "disquiet," "painful emotion marked by alarm," and "anxious concern," can also mean "to doubt," "to distrust," "to lose hope," and even "to be in apprehension of evil." Being seized or educated (i.e., *apprehended*) by fear makes it impossible to feel or know Love because we have resigned ourselves to evil, making evil a guest of honor at the table. Being fearful is doubting Love's allness.

Fear is the exact opposite of Love, and thus fear blocks us from loving and being loved. Fear blocks us from making decisions, from being well, from helping others, from realizing our full potential, from all that is good. Fear makes it impossible to perceive the true self. It is always evil's goal to deceive, to thwart, to lie, to keep us from feeling Love — to keep us from knowing what's real.

Why do you think the Bible contains the phrase "fear not" 84 times? This is not merely a command telling us not to be afraid. Let's dig deeper to see the spiritual significance: "Fear not" literally tells us that *fear can't be.* When Love, which is *all,* is recognized, that means fear can't exist.[1] Fear melts away, is pushed out as extraneous, and is seen as nothing. Then we can know for certain that we are safe.

On the other hand, why does the Bible often tell us to *fear God?* In this context, the word *fear* denotes "honor," "awe," "respect," and "reverence," rather than fright or dread. We can find our courage by replacing being afraid with being reverent. This shift in our perception immediately brings clarity, and helps us to be more respectful and loving in any difficult situation.

For instance, I once had to call a customer service representative about an error on my telephone bill that had gone on for over a year. The phone company was threatening cutoff for this overdue portion, even though I had been refusing to pay it because it was the company's mistake. At first I was very fearful I wouldn't be able to present my case properly without blowing up (after all, I had put it off for such a long time, and now I had no choice). After silencing my fear through prayer I asked for guidance. I finally picked up the phone with a loving and respectful attitude towards the person on the other end. Instead of assuming I would be dealing with an idiot who was going to ignore me, I honored that person's integrity, expecting the Law of Principle to prevail. And that's exactly what happened. The person understood my story without question and reversed the charges immediately.

Replacing fear with respect can work in dangerous situations as well. It is an extremely effective way to diffuse potentially explosive situations. I was once threatened with bodily harm, and overcame my fear by shouting back, "I refuse to accept this lie about you. There is *only love* right here!" The man wept and fled.

Spiritual teacher Gangaji reminds us that if we meet resistance with more resistance, we will never know freedom from fear. What we perceive as fear is actually a door opening to all the answers we seek. Once we face the fear head-on, we will discover that fear is nothing.[2]

Hatred Has No Legitimacy

"Hatreds do not ever cease in this world by hating, but by love; this is an eternal truth." — the Buddha[3]

Another of Love's opposites — the one we usually think of — is hate. The word *hate* comes from the Old Saxon *hatan,* "to be hostile"; the Greek word is *kedos,* meaning "trouble," and "sorrow." One of Webster's definitions calls hate an "emotion of intense aversion, usually springing from *anger, fear,* or a sense of injury; also *an emotional habit,* or *attitude of mind,* in which aversion is coupled with *settled ill will.*" Thus hatred is a *dis-eased habitual way of thinking* — which can be reversed at any time should a person choose to do so.

Hate cannot exist in the face of Love. No matter what the despots of the world may say or do, no matter how terrorists may attempt to instill fear (and thus encourage more hate), human hatred has no legitimacy, no mandate of its own.[4] Whenever we experience hatred — either recognizing hate rising up in our own personal behavior, or having to deal with hate from someone else — the mightiest weapon we have is Love.

This powerful idea isn't new. A biblical saying tells us that "hatred stirs up strife, but Love covers all sins" (see Proverbs 10:12). When we treat others as we want to be treated, each of us is a living extension of Love. We can awaken to our connectedness in the One Mind to everyone and everything else. We are then expressing and applying in a practical way the Law of Love's power over every adversity and injustice — erasing sin. Jesus taught, "Do unto others as you would have them do to you" (Luke 6:31, NIV). The Buddha put it even more succinctly: "Consider others as yourself."[5]

Certainly hatred is the opposite of loving one's neighbor as oneself. Often hatred is met with more hatred. We may want to react to heinous acts of malice or violence with rage, grief, and revenge. But retaliation breeds only *more* hatred, not less.

In the 1997 sci-fi parable *The Fifth Element* (a film written and directed by Luc Besson), in the 23rd century a caliginous planet of fire is headed towards Earth. The entity is discovered to be "pure evil," whose only purpose is to destroy all life. When the world's leader sends weapons to attack and annihilate the entity, instead of sustaining damage it increases in size and intensity. The fact is, evil always thrives on acts of evil. Enter Leeloo (played by Milla Jovovich), a "supreme being," who has come "to protect all life."

Only a very few learned priests are left on the planet who possess the divine knowledge passed down from generation to generation in case just such a crisis should come to pass. One of these men is Vito Cornelius (Ian Holm), who recognizes Leeloo's power and knows how to speak her language — a divine tongue "spoken throughout the universe before time was time." Korben Dallas (Bruce Willis), hapless cabdriver and former member of the elite special forces unit of the federated army, meets Cornelius and becomes reluctantly involved with Leeloo and the plan to save the world. After many misadventures, in the final moments of the film — when it appears there is nothing that can be done to stop the evil — Leeloo has become despondent, exhausted, and doubtful that there is anything on Earth worth saving. Dallas convinces her that "Love is worth saving" and finally confesses his love for her. At the instant of their kiss, the evil is stopped dead in its tracks, only 62 miles out, just as it is about to hit Earth's outer atmosphere.[6] Finally, the lesson we must learn is simple: It's Love Itself that saves the planet.

Mary Baker Eddy says it plainly: "Love is the liberator."[7] When Love is recognized and embraced, even in the most horrific situation, circumstances can change in a moment, and healing can take place. Love gives unconditionally, even when there is no response. Look at the examples of civil disobedience inspired by Mahatma Ghandi in India and Martin Luther King Jr. in the United States. Hatred and injustice were unmasked and eventually destroyed — not by war, but by Love.

Further, Love's abiding power cannot be extinguished by assassins' bullets. A perfect case in point is Christ Jesus, who accepted crucifixion, the gruesome capital punishment of his day, even though he'd committed no crime. In so doing, with his death and resurrection he showed everyone that Love was not only the victor over hate, but even more potent than death itself. (Whether you believe that Jesus' death and resurrection are historical fact or legend, Love's lesson is the same.) One of the things we can learn from Jesus' example is that even in the most grievous situations, we can choose to love more.

Daniel Biwila of the Republic of Congo, during the time of his country's civil war, was talking with his friend in a shop when a stranger entered and pointed a gun at his friend's head, and then at Biwila's head. They were both forced to kneel. Keeping the first two of the Ten Commandments (see Exodus 20) in his thought ("Thou shalt have no other gods before me" and "Thou shalt not make unto thee any graven image,.... Thou shalt not bow down thyself to them, nor serve them") Biwila silently prayed "to see only God's man present — not one with a gun intending to do harm." The aggressor's attitude soon became less menacing. "I saw that to bow down to this gunman was like bowing to a 'graven image,' an idol," Biwila recounts.

"And I thought to myself, 'What's attributing power to this gun? Was it the finger, the arm — or the carnal mind? And what is causing this man to act this way?'" Biwila chose to hold to the fact that "man is governed by God, divine Love. The image of this Love cannot depart from the straight line of perfection, and that included this man."

Even though the man's finger was still on the trigger, Biwila continued along these lines in silent prayer, reasoning that "God being almighty, infinite Love, how can His spiritual expression, His image and likeness, deviate from His government?" As Biwila continued praying, he noticed "a tinge of kindness in the voice of the man. He put down his gun and murmured, 'Are you not afraid?' Then without any other word, he stepped aside and moved to the door. My friend stood up, and together we recovered our liberty."[8]

George G. Ritchie, MD, tells of a man he met in 1945 at the end of World War II when Ritchie was part of a team assigned to a concentration camp near Wuppertal to help give medical assistance to the newly liberated prisoners. The American soldiers at the camp called the man "Wild Bill Cody" because of his handlebar mustache and the fact that his Polish name was too difficult to pronounce. Although Ritchie guessed that Cody had been an inmate at the camp for only a short time due to his relatively healthy appearance, Cody had already settled in as camp translator because he spoke five languages fluently. Not only that, Cody also was trusted to arbitrate all sorts of disputes, and seemed able to peaceably resolve every squabble among men of so many different nationalities. Amazingly enough, every faction of the camp looked upon Cody as a friend. Although Cody worked sixteen-hour days, he showed no signs of fatigue, nor was he gaunt from starvation the way most of the other inmates were. Ritchie says Cody's "compassion for his fellow prisoners glowed on his face, and it was to this glow that I came when my own spirits were low." Cody was his team's "greatest asset, reasoning with the different groups, counseling forgiveness." One day over tea, Ritchie mentioned how difficult it is to choose to forgive. At this point Cody told Ritchie his own story:

> "We lived in the Jewish section of Warsaw,...my wife, our two daughters, and our three little boys. When the Germans reached our street they lined everyone against a wall and opened up with machine guns. I begged to be allowed to die with my family, but because I spoke German they put me in a work group....
>
> "I had to decide right then," he continued, "whether to let myself hate the soldiers who had done this. It was an easy decision, really. I was a lawyer. In my practice I had seen too often what hate could do to people's minds and bodies. Hate

had just killed the six people who mattered most to me in the world. I decided then that I would spend the rest of my life — whether it was a few days or many years — loving every person I came in contact with."[9]

Ritchie also learned that Cody had lived at the camp since 1939. "For six years he had lived on the same starvation diet, slept in the same airless and disease-ridden barracks as everyone else, but without the least physical or mental deterioration." Ritchie realized that "'Loving every person,'" was the power that had kept Cody well despite every deprivation he had endured.[10]

When we choose to express Love in the face of hate, we will bring harmony where there was once chaos. Hatred and evil cannot survive in the Light of Love's Truth; they must shrivel and die as sure as the Wicked Witch of the West melted away when Dorothy drenched her with a bucket of water.

Compassion — An Unselfed Love

"To put the world in order, we must first put the nation in order; to put the nation in order, we must put the family in order; to put the family in order, we must first cultivate our personal life; to cultivate our personal life, we must first set our hearts right." — Confucius[11]

Eliminating hatred, we are free from the burden of blaming others, keeping score, and the false sense that our own separate ego is in control. When we express this "unselfed love" — where no personal ego is involved — this brings spiritual understanding, and healing will result. Whatever keeps our thought in line with unselfed love directly receives the Divine power.[12] Then we are able to see that there is only One Ego, not many. Knowing this fact enables us to have more compassion for others — because loving one's neighbor *is* loving oneself (One Self).

Behind the meaning of *compassion* are the ideas of "forgiveness," "mercy," "patience," "condolence," "sympathy," "tenderness," "turning away from wrath," and "rendering blessing for evil." In Hindu and Buddhist traditions, all actions that alleviate the suffering of others express *karuna* (Sanskrit for compassion), which along with *prajna* (wisdom) is a stepping-stone to enlightenment.[13] The concept of compassion — "suffering with" others — should not be confused with pitying them or taking on their problems; instead the goal is to *remove* the suffering.

In biblical accounts, Jesus is often said to have shown compassion on others before healing them. The Greek verb used in the Gospels is *splagchnizesthai,* "to be moved with compassion," which comes from the noun *splagchna,* referring to the heart, lungs, liver, and intestines; in other words, this compassion moves a person to what the ancient Greeks called the very depths of one's being.[14] Why is compassion so essential? I think because it is a powerful way of seeing our true identity as God's children — our literal connectedness to everyone and everything in our common divine childhood. Those who suffer are suffering precisely because they don't feel particularly loved nor cared for. Whenever we suffer, we experience a feeling of separateness that is often profoundly overwhelming. If you've been there before and found your way out, your ability to know and share that same Love that brought you back helps bring healing to others.

Forgiveness — The Way To Freedom

> "Hatred is a banquet until you recognize you are the main course." — Herbert Benson[15]

It's common knowledge that we can't change something that's already happened. But we *can* change how we *think* about it. We can decide whether or not we're going to lug around a past hurt as a burden or legacy, as a tragedy or responsibility — or, instead chalk it up as a lesson to help us grow stronger. Forgiveness — a letting go of all past suffering — is the way to freedom. Without forgiveness, suffering will continue.

What if the person who has wronged us doesn't deserve to be forgiven? What if that person has not changed? The point is, regardless of whether someone can or will acknowledge wrongdoing, once we can forgive, a great burden will be lifted, and we will experience healing. Welsh poet George Herbert (1593–1633) echoed the words of Chinese sage Confucius when he wrote: "he who cannot forgive another breaks the bridge over which he must pass himself."[16]

The response to sin isn't to impose an ever-stricter code of behavior; it is to know God.[17] Truly, what person among us actually merits forgiveness? When Jesus was asked by some Pharisees (fellow leaders of a Jewish sect of his time) to condemn to death a woman caught in the act of adultery, his response was, "He who is without sin among you, let him first cast a stone at her," and of course, the sheepish crowd straggled away. Then he said to the woman: "Go and sin no more." Jesus spoke again to them saying, "I am the light of the world: Anyone who follows me shall not walk in darkness but have the light of life" (see John 8:1–12). By this statement, I don't think Jesus was asking others to follow him as a human leader or as a Messiah, nor was he claiming that he was God; rather I think he meant: "Love is Light; if you forgive others in the same way that I have forgiven this woman, you will no longer suffer, wandering in the darkness of sin, but you will know this Light for yourself."

Light indicates not only such ideas as warmth (fire), illumination (inspiration), or clarity (shedding light on something), but also buoyancy. That is, we feel *light*er when we let go of the heavy baggage of sin (either the sins of others or our own). This is more of the en*light*enment I mentioned earlier in the chapter on the Law of Spirit. When someone is able to recognize that *sin isn't part of anyone's nature,* it's a lot easier to forgive. Remember, we can throw out the counterfeit a lot quicker when we know the Truth. That's how Jesus healed: When others saw a sinful mortal that needed fixing, Jesus perceived instead a perfect individual, already pure and whole. In this perfect individual he saw God's own likeness, and this correct view instantly healed the sick.[18] Jesus never blamed people — nor their parents, heredity, environment, status, or circumstances — he just healed them!

Peter, a disciple of Jesus, once asked his teacher how often we ought to forgive sin — "seven times?" he wondered. Jesus answered, "seventy times seven." (The use of sevens is symbolic here; in Bible language and in much ancient wisdom, the number 7 implies infinity, completeness, or totality.)[19] Jesus then told Peter the story of a servant who was forgiven a debt of 10,000 bucks which he'd owed to the king, yet he went right out and threw his *own* friend in prison when the friend couldn't pay back the *one* dollar owed *him.* When the king heard about this he scolded the servant: "Shouldn't you have compassion on your fellowservant, just as I had on you?" The king then decided to deliver the servant to the tormentors, until the servant would pay all that was due to him. Jesus explained: "So likewise shall my heavenly Father do also to you, if you don't forgive from your hearts everyone their trespasses" (see Matthew 18:21–35). What was Jesus really saying here? I don't think he was talking about keeping score on how many times we should forgive, nor was he saying that God is a tyrant like the king in the story, punishing us when we get out of line. The point is, we are advised to forgive an infinite number of times; and the forgiveness must be authentic (from our hearts). Otherwise, we ourselves will be tormented continually — because *not* to forgive is to disregard our Divine Source (our heavenly Father-Mother). In other words, a lack of forgiveness on our part logically leads to our own suffering. Eddy describes God's chastisement (which can only be loving) this way: "Love will force you to accept what best promotes your growth."[20]

Perhaps the most amazing story of forgiveness comes from Christ Jesus, who, while enduring the indignity of crucifixion, actually asked God to forgive those who had condemned him to death: "Forgive them, for they don't know what they're doing" (see Luke 23:34). The common interpretation of the story of Jesus' death and resurrection is that he came to Earth to serve as our Savior, a sort of ultimate sacrificial lamb to pay for the sins of all mankind for all time; then he rose from the dead in order to show us that he was God in the flesh. But as mentioned earlier, once we know that God is All, then we know we are not "fallen" or separate from God — so this explanation doesn't even make sense.

Here's the quandary: if Jesus were God, then he'd have to be sinless, and in that case, how could he even *have* compassion, since he couldn't *know* suffering? If he experienced suffering, then he wouldn't be God. Infinity cannot be enclosed in a finite fleshly package. So the paradox goes in circles.

Or, let's take Jesus out of the picture. If God is All and that makes evil unreal, then why should God care one iota about us? Our experience seems so unworthy of a Deity even bothering to know what's happening to us — which would make prayer useless. With this scenario, we would be back to an anthropomorphic Mount Olympus type of God — a Zeus creating, *containing,* and *knowing* evil — hurling random tragedies at us hapless mortals.

How do we escape this seemingly endless duality? Simply by realizing the allness of God. This means that Jesus was here to tell us that the Christ Consciousness is reflected *in each of us,* not just in one particularly renowned rabbi named Jesus. And, it means that forgiveness and healing come whenever we disavow evil as powerless. Eddy, in answer to the question "Is Sin Forgiven?" untangles it beautifully:

> The law of Life and Truth is the law of [the] Christ, destroying all sense of sin and death. It does more than forgive the false sense named sin, for it pursues and punishes it, and will not let sin go until it is destroyed — *until nothing is left to be forgiven, to suffer, or to be punished.* Forgiven thus, sickness and sin have no relapse. God's law reaches and destroys evil by virtue of the allness of God.
>
> *God need not know the evil God destroys,* any more than the legislator need know the criminal who is punished by the law enacted. God's law is in three words, "I am All"; and this perfect law is ever present to rebuke any claim of another law. *God pities our woes with the love of a Parent for a child — not by becoming human, and knowing sin, or naught, but by removing our knowledge of what is not. God could not destroy our woes totally if God possessed any knowledge of them.* God's sympathy is divine, not human. It is Truth's knowledge of its own infinitude which forbids the genuine existence of even a *claim* to error. This knowledge is light wherein there is no darkness — *not light holding darkness within itself.* The consciousness of light is like the eternal law of God, revealing God and nothing else.[21]

It's clear that in order to forgive and be free, it is necessary to release the hurt and anger utterly. The word *forgive* offers us the richness of multiple meanings, which include "to grant completely and overwhelmingly," "to cease to indulge or entertain," "to send away," and "to give up a claim on account of a wrong committed." In Greek the word is *aphiemi*, indicating such definitions as "to send forth," "to lay aside," "to let alone," "to omit," "to set at liberty," "to yield," and "to relieve." The Hebrew word *nâsâ* adds such shades of meaning as "to advance," "to arise," "to lift," "to ease," and even "to exalt (self)," "to raise up," and "to respect."[22] It's vital that we expunge the record. Wipe the slate clean. Trash the grudges, the mistakes, the blunders, even the deep wounds and regrets, and go forward, pure in heart. Not whitewashed. But pure through and through. When we know that each of us is inherently pure already, forgiveness is not as difficult.

Healer Kathleen Clemenson describes forgiveness as a replacement — or "giving for" — process. She explains that to forgive is to *replace* blame, anger, bad behavior, resentment, etc. *with Godlike qualities*.[23] For instance, we can apply any of the seven synonyms for God to the person we want to forgive (Check the lists at the back of each chapter and break out the thesaurus for more ideas on finding just the right words in a particular situation to describe God's qualities). Of course, forgiveness is often difficult, because we're angry, hurt, and feeling justified. There may not be even one thing we can think of to like about this particular person. Yet when we let go of our own ego as well as any notion of ego in the other person, asking to *see what God sees*, certainly something new will be revealed. Choosing to share the divine childhood together as equals under God's care, forgiveness can begin. When we make even a small attempt to do this, the healings that result can be remarkable. Stubbornness can be viewed as Principle, loyalty, or idealism. Self-destructive behavior can be seen through — as a search for self-realization, Soul-existence.

Someone very dear to me was abusing drugs; I hardly recognized him — the guy I knew seemed to have almost disappeared. Yet when he asked for a place to stay, I decided I would at least make a sincere effort to see the pure and innocent child of God — not a mortal who had made some very unwise choices and suffered for them. In my prayer I refused to see the disconnected agitation he was displaying, and held only to the loving, sensitive, spirited man I knew he still was. Within two days he had come back to himself. This was a new beginning, and I was grateful. Even when this kind of difficult healing process takes months — or even years — the burdens lifted, the spiritual growth, and the Love discovered and shared are always worth it.

When we decide not to forgive, our continuing anger directed at others is often a manifestation of our own fear turned outward. Without realizing it, we can project our own feelings of guilt or inadequacy onto others. But such bitterness is so much wasted energy; we must forgive — even when the person who has hurt us doesn't ask for forgiveness; otherwise we'll remain perpetually bound to the wrongdoer, imprisoned by our own anger and pain.[24]

I've found over and over again that a physical complaint is the manifestation of a problem that needs to be addressed. Whether an ailment is a little nudge or a major wake-up call, it's an opportunity to pray — and prayer always brings good results. Once I got a splinter in my foot, and I couldn't for the life of me pull it out with tweezers; it just seemed to be too far into the skin. I asked God to take care of it: "I leave it up to You now — I can't do it!" The foot was a bit painful but I could still walk on it, so I didn't really think about it much. Later I was having an argument with my husband, wishing it would end, and all of a sudden I realized I truly needed to forgive myself for being so inflexible that day, and also to forgive him for being so overbearing at that moment. I didn't say anything, but at that very instant I felt a strange sensation in my foot, like little electrical pulses. I remembered the splinter and started to smile. Soon our point of contention was resolved. I don't have to tell you that when I went to look at my foot, there was the splinter — it had worked its way out. I was able to remove it easily.

We can't resolve a relationship problem by attacking the other person's defenses. Instead, we have to tear down our own defenses.[25] When we embrace ourselves and others in Love, recognizing Love's allness, then all mistakes are eradicated. Forgiving is *not* condoning or excusing wrongdoing, but *dismissing* the evil in order to give the real individual — God's child — a place to be. If other people refuse to repent, that's not our fault, but at least we can be free ourselves, and wish them well in the journey towards realizing their own inevitable freedom. Forgiveness means we can finally move forward, putting history behind us for good — and only *for* the Good!

There Is Only This Moment

"Yesterday is history. Tomorrow is a mystery. Today is a gift.
That's why we call it the present." — Babatunde Olatunje[26]

What is *history*? And why should we attach it to our identity? The word *history* is defined as a "narrative of events" either real or imaginary, "a tale," or "story." History is also "the branch of knowledge that records and explains past events as steps in human progress." If you think you can or can't do certain things because of your history, think again. History is what we make it. Historians reconsider and revise history all the time. And we can do the same with our own lives.

History simply consists of the stories we tell ourselves and each other about who we are. Eddy says: "The true theory of the universe, including man, is not in material history but in spiritual development."[27] Her vision is not just theoretical, but a real possibility we can experience here and now.

German physicist Hermann Weyl says, "The world does not happen, it simply is."[28] More than one physicist admits that it is time for us to give up our mechanistic thinking about the universe and embrace the new paradigm of only consciousness. Fred Alan Wolf, quantum physicist, says that the concepts of matter, space, and time are breaking down. Weyl adds that "the idea that time 'flows,' or that the present moment somehow moves from the past to the future in time, has no place in the physicist's description of the world."[29] Wolf explains that there is a mathematical basis for stating that one-way causality (cause *preceding* effect) is not necessarily true. In other words, it is actually possible for the *future* to influence the *present*; and therefore we can develop our acuity to know the future, just as we already know the past. Saul-Paul Sirag, another well-known physicist, goes so far as to say that *we can re-create the past* because "there really is no fixed solid past.... there is only the now."[30] Sirag describes the multidimensions of hyperspace as the "Cosmic Mind," and says that the structure of physics is simply the structure of the One Mind. Sirag also says the body is only a projection from this greater Mind: "We're living in a 3-D movie," he said in 1987. As we accept this idea, Sirag went on, in the future we'll learn to "make our own movies," i.e., to live life more consciously.[31]

This motion-picture model was explored by Paramahansa Yogananda some forty years earlier. He wrote:

> Just as cinematic images appear to be real but are only combinations of light and shade, so is the universal variety a delusive seeming.... One's values are profoundly changed when he is finally convinced that creation is only a vast motion picture; and that not in it, but beyond it, lies his own reality.
>
> After I had finished writing this chapter, I sat on my bed in the lotus posture. My room was dimly lit by two shaded lamps. Lifting my gaze, I noticed that the ceiling was dotted with small mustard-colored lights, scintillating and quivering with a radiumlike luster. Myriads of penciled rays, like sheets of rain, gathered into a transparent shaft and poured silently upon me.
>
> At once my physical body lost its grossness and became metamorphosed into astral texture. I felt a floating sensation as, barely touching the bed, the weightless body shifted slightly and alternately to left and right. I looked around the room; the

furniture and walls were as usual, but the little mass of light had so multiplied that the ceiling was invisible. I was wonder-struck.

"This is the cosmic motion-picture mechanism." A Voice spoke as though from within the light. "Shedding its beam on the white screen of your bed sheets, it is producing the picture of your body. Behold, your form is nothing but light!"....

For a long time I experienced this motion picture of my body in the faintly lit theater of my own bedroom. Though I have had many visions, none was ever more singular. As the illusion of a solid body was completely dissipated,...my realization deepened that the essence of all objects is light....[32]

In the 21st century, that future is already here. And of course, it's always been here![33] Trying to heal using anything other than scientific prayer is like poking at a movie screen when a film is out of focus, instead of going directly to the projectionist to correct the problem.

Dr. Deepak Chopra often utilizes in his medical practice the ancient Hindu philosophy of India, which he calls Vedic Science. He says the past, present, and future are all "properties of consciousness. The past is recollection, memory; the future is anticipation; the present is awareness. Therefore time is *the movement of thought*. Both past and future are born in the imagination; only the present, which is awareness, is real and eternal."[34]

In our common experience, however, everyone supposedly has a material past. So what is "the past"? What does it reveal, if anything? Of course, one definition of *past* is "elapsed," "preceding," and "bygone," as in "a time gone by." But also *past* can mean "beyond" or "reach and go beyond a point near at hand"; in this sense, the past is exactly the same as the future! When you look at it this way, it's a lot easier to leave the past behind! Keep in mind that *bygone* also means *outmoded*, which in one sense means "no longer acceptable, current, or usable; made unfashionable or obsolete." When you view your own past in this light, just what has preceded the present moment? Has time? Not really, since time is only a human construct.

When we are stuck in material finite thinking, stubbornly trying to hold Infinitude in the grasp of matter, we limit Love, we squander Love.[35] The past, like the future, is truly beyond our grasp. And what a blessing this is: We can reasonably let go of our futile hold on past hurts, resentments, and failures, as well as all fears and expectations about future events. This detachment — this letting go — will make room for Love to prevail.

The truth is, every moment we have a choice. Each of us can decide for ourselves what is no longer acceptable or usable. We can decide that the only thing that has ever come before or will come after this moment is the fullness of Life, Goodness, and promise. Love's promises were fulfilled, are fulfilled, will be fulfilled.

What will you do with this moment? Hold onto the wounds of the past, or let go, forgive, and accept and share the endless possibilities for Love that exist right here and now? Each moment you have is a gift from God — and you can make it a gift to yourself, as well as a gift to bring healing to someone else — even in the smallest ways. If someone else doesn't have a smile, give that person one of yours. Share what you have with *everyone* you meet!

There Are No Enemies

> "When we wait patiently on God and seek Truth righteously, [God] directs our path.... to *begin* aright and to continue the strife of demonstrating the great problem of being, is doing much." — Mary Baker Eddy[36]

Jesus, Muhammad, and other great prophets and teachers have advised us to love our enemies. In an essay entitled *Love Your Enemies,* Mary Baker Eddy begins:

> Who is thine enemy that thou shouldst love him? Is it a creature or a thing outside thine own creation?
>
> Can you see an enemy, except you first formulate this enemy and then look upon the object of your own conception? What is it that harms you? Can height, or depth, or any other creature separate you from the Love that is omnipresent good, — that blesses infinitely one and all? Simply count your enemy to be that which defiles, defaces, and dethrones the Christ-image that you should reflect.[37]

Keep your focus on the real individual (both yourself and your neighbor), and, Eddy says, you will see that "'Love thine enemies' is identical with 'Thou hast no enemies.'"[38] She continues:

> The present is ours; the future, big with events. Every man and woman should be to-day a law to himself, herself — a law of loyalty to Jesus' Sermon on the Mount....
>
> We should measure our love for God by our love for man; and our sense of Science will be measured by our obedience to God — fulfilling the law of Love, doing good to all; imparting, so far as we reflect them, Truth, Life, and Love to all within the radius of our atmosphere of thought.[39]

Dr. Chopra might say that this fulfillment of the Law of Love is the development of an awareness of the true self (i.e., not of one's own ego, nor of a conflict with the ego of another, but a coming to an awareness of the One Self) — waking up in what he calls "the state of self-referral."[40] And where else would we want to be? When we put this view into practice in our daily lives, we can learn to let go of and transform any past hurt — blessing everyone around us in the process.

It is even possible for us to pray for tyrants such as Kim Jong-Il or terrorists like Osama bin Laden. Whether we are able to comprehend it or not, Omniscient Love knows these men are pure and perfect in their divine childhood. If we pray to ask for just a tiny glimpse of this fact, our prayers for our enemies are powerful. No one is outside of All-encompassing Love, and therefore no one is beyond the possibility of repentance. Even if people are deluded, actually praying to God for support to kill themselves and others, Love is still telling them the Truth — and thus their awakening to spiritual awareness remains possible.

Indeed the Apostle Paul initially was a terrorist: In his warped thinking, Saul (his given name) felt totally justified in his work to exterminate Christians, and he was supported by Rome to carry out brutal acts against them. Yet on a trip to Damascus to persecute more Christians, he was struck blind and then healed — by a member of the group that he had come to take captive (see Acts chapter 9). His conversion to Christianity (when he took the name Paul) was not only a spiritual revelation for him personally; the work he accomplished after that changed the whole world. Paul's story has considerable relevance today because it promises us that even terrorists can wake up to the error of their ways and become God's instruments for peace. A *Christian Science Monitor* writer points out:

> Today's terrorists, no more than Saul, don't operate in a vacuum. What was the mental climate in which Saul was operating? What were the intended victims of his hatred doing?
>
> There's no doubt that Saul's victims were aware of their danger and were praying, and there is little doubt about how they were praying. They were disciples of Jesus, and he had taught them to "pray for them which despitefully use you and persecute you" (Matthew 5:44)....
>
> Isn't it logical that this kind of praying being done by Saul's intended victims had something to do with his epiphany? Doesn't the prayer for deliverance from evil include both protection

from evil and freedom from doing evil's bidding? Saul must have been yearning, praying for the success of his mission, mistaken though it was. As often happens when one's sense of right is not clear, Saul was pushing his resolve with self-will. His real desire to serve God, however, and the disciples' desire to serve God naturally coincided. The result was not anyone's manipulating or controlling another, but the higher law of the God that is Love prevailing....

As we continue to pray, may we not expect members of the Al Qaeda network to experience epiphanies and be changed? This is not a naive assumption, but a recognition of the power of prayer. Such prayer that God's will be done will also equip us to guide and comfort those awakening from their delusions and misinformation as they readjust their lives to serve the purpose of peace on earth....

Every individual revelation of God's goodness and supremacy changes one's actions and character. It contributes to the world's emergence from considering murder and suicide as a tool, to valuing each human life and working to elevate and preserve it.[41]

No prayer is ever in vain. Our daily prayers for our most bitter enemies can and will prove to be the most powerful of all.

In the Gospel of Matthew, right before Jesus declared that we ought to love our enemies, he started out with one of the most famous speeches ever made, based on familiar Jewish sayings he'd been reciting in Hebrew (and probably singing in Aramaic) for years — what Christians today call the Sermon on the Mount (Matthew 5:1–17; 38–48; Matthew 5–7 is all of it):

And seeing the multitudes, he went up into a mountain: and when he was set, his disciples came unto him:

And he opened his mouth, and taught them, saying,

Blessed are the poor in spirit: for theirs is the kingdom of heaven.

Blessed are they that mourn: for they shall be comforted.

Blessed are the meek: for they shall inherit the earth.

Blessed are they which do hunger and thirst after righteousness: for they shall be filled.

Blessed are the merciful: for they shall obtain mercy.

Blessed are the pure in heart: for they shall see God.

Blessed are the peacemakers: for they shall be called the children of God.

Blessed are they which are persecuted for righteousness' sake: for theirs is the kingdom of heaven.

Blessed are ye, when men shall revile you, and persecute you, and shall say all manner of evil against you falsely, for my sake. Rejoice, and be exceeding glad: for great is your reward in heaven: for so persecuted they the prophets which were before you.

Ye are the salt of the earth: but if the salt have lost his savour, wherewith shall it be salted? it is thenceforth good for nothing, but to be cast out, and to be trodden under foot of men.

Ye are the light of the world. A city that is set on an hill cannot be hid. Neither do men light a candle, and put it under a bushel, but on a candlestick; and it giveth light unto all that are in the house.

Let your light so shine before men, that they may see your good works, and glorify your Father which is in heaven.

Think not that I am come to destroy the law, or the prophets: I am not come to destroy, but to fulfil....

Ye have heard that it hath been said, An eye for an eye, and a tooth for a tooth: But I say unto you, That ye resist not evil: but whosoever shall smite thee on thy right cheek, turn to him the other also. And if any man will sue thee at the law, and take away thy coat, let him have thy cloak also. And whosoever shall compel thee to go a mile, go with him twain. Give to him that asketh thee, and from him that would borrow of thee turn not thou away.

Ye have heard that it hath been said, Thou shalt love thy neighbour, and hate thine enemy. But I say unto you, Love your enemies, bless them that curse you, do good to them that hate you, and pray for them which despitefully use you, and persecute you; that ye may be the children of your Father which is in heaven: for he maketh his sun to rise on the evil and on the good, and sendeth rain on the just and on the unjust.

For if ye love them which love you, what reward have ye? do not even the publicans the same? And if ye salute your brethren only, what do ye more than others? do not even the publicans so? Be ye therefore perfect, even as your Father which is in heaven is perfect.

When we look at Jesus' final command in this passage — "to be perfect" — from a spiritual perspective rather than a material one, it makes a lot more sense. When we're recognizing and obeying the Law of Love, we see that each of us is perfect, because our Father-Mother-Source in Spirit is perfect. And if perfection is so, it's true for everyone.

Let's not confuse *perfection* with *perfectionism*. Perfectionism, grounded in materiality, is a habit of judgment that condemns each of us continually, because if we are mortals, we can never be perfect — and thus we're doomed to perpetual failure. Perfectionism is actually a refusal to let ourselves move forward, and "a pursuit of the worst in ourselves, the part that tells us that nothing we do will ever be good enough."[42] Once we see that we're *spiritual* individuals expressing Love's Infinity, we awaken to our *innate* perfection — something we never have to work for to complete, because it's already done. Then perfectionism is an irrational and harmful habit we can abandon once and for all. Once our true spiritual nature is established in our own thought, we can also reach out to others and heal all kinds of situations, not just our own. Then having any sort of a quarrel with anybody seems laughable. Why fight against *our own life,* going against the One Self, trying to defy the entire universe? When we know the reality of being, we don't have to battle anyone or anything.

We can also cultivate a sense of humor about the things and people that bother us! Break the tension with an observation of what is really happening, and give yourself (and the other guy) a break from all the grief. Love wants us to laugh and be joyful. Even the word *wit* (meaning both "intellectual power" as well as "clever expression") comes from the Middle English *witen,* "I know," akin to the Gothic *witan,* "to observe," and the Latin *videre,* "to see," which goes all the way back to the Sanskrit root *vid,* "to know, to learn" (from which comes the word *veda,* "I know").[43] So when we choose to *witness* our true selves (the One Self), we are knowing all people as Love knows us. One of the Ten Commandments (see Exodus 20:1–17) is not to "bear false witness" against one's neighbor. As a child I was taught this meant we shouldn't tell a lie. But the implications are so much more than that. Let us choose to witness God's perfect child instead of a flawed mortal counterfeit. Let us "bear true witness" and see real spiritual individuals — we're members of one family sharing our divine childhood. This knowledge and understanding puts Love into action. It's heartening to discover that the Old High German word, *minna,* which is where we get the word "mind," actually means "love." Love is the Intelligence that gives us the spiritual truths we need to know, setting us free from every limitation.

The Answer Is Love

"The epoch approaches when the understanding of the truth of being will be the basis of true religion. At present mortals progress slowly for fear of being thought ridiculous. They are slaves to fashion, pride, and sense. Sometime we shall learn how Spirit, the great architect, has created men and women in Science. We ought to weary of the fleeting and false and to cherish nothing which hinders our highest selfhood." — Mary Baker Eddy[44]

I am not about to tell you that the Twin Towers didn't really collapse, that the German Holocaust never happened, that there was no genocide in Rwanda, or that your great-great-great grandmother is not dead. I am not going to tell you that you haven't experienced whatever pain or joy it is that you know you have experienced. I do not want to belittle common experience. That is not the point.

I will tell you this: No matter how horrible we think we've got it, no matter how bad a hand each of us may have been dealt, and no matter how many catastrophes we see around us... *Love is telling us right now and perpetually that ALL IS WELL.*

A single mother was struggling financially with two small children. She had been asking God for direction, asking in prayer to be shown how to do more than just focus on her own outlining. She went to sleep one night in this prayerful frame of mind. Suddenly she was awakened from a sound sleep by someone touching her; as she came to consciousness she could see a man on her bed on his knees. A huge wave of fear came over her as the danger of the situation dawned on her. This stranger threatened to kill her if she spoke up, and made it clear he was going to rape her. Then the woman remembered that her daughter had climbed into bed next to her earlier in the evening. She knew she had to stay quiet to protect her daughter. As the woman's thoughts raced she soon realized there was nothing she could do to stop this man. At that moment, she surrendered to God:

I understood that God is Love — to the depth of my being. That's what I surrendered to.

As I did this, it felt almost like a physical shield went up — starting from the top of my head and coming over my body, just like a gentle wave, replacing the waves of fear. It just ran down my body.

This intruder who had brought with him this atmosphere of

hate, got up off my bed. Leaned over. And kissed me on the cheek. And he left. He didn't rape me. He just left.[45]

The Power of Love is unsurpassed. It isn't surprising that in study after study, love has been found to be vital to our health. In a study at the University of Miami, premature infants were stroked three times a day for ten minutes. As Dr. Chopra relates, the report described this nurturing for preemies as "kinesthetic tactile stimulation — God forbid call it love." Still, those babies gained an average of 49% in weight *per day* given the same diet as the other babies who were not held.[46]

Whatever your question is, the answer is Love.

Wake up now in this moment, and see what Love sees! I guarantee your life will radically change — some problems will disappear in an instant; others will fade away only after a mighty struggle — but through it all, Love is our refuge and strength, our Guide and Protector. Love heals all wounds and brings wholeness.

Paying Our Proper Debt

"Owe no man any thing, but to love one another: for he that
loveth another hath fulfilled the law." (Romans 13:8)

Interestingly enough, the opposite of Love is also debt. This indicates to us another opportunity for forgiveness and healing. In the standard prayer Jesus provides (see Matthew 6:9–13 for The Lord's Prayer), there is one line that's been translated into English two different ways. It goes: "...and forgive us our debts, as we forgive our debtors" or "...and forgive us our trespasses, as we forgive those who trespass against us." This description of mutual respect demonstrates The Law of Love: Since Love is All, debt (or transgression, sin, fault, violation) is nothing — for both you and me. Because we can affirm this Truth together with conviction, we can honestly forgive. Forgiveness works naturally in a circle, just like that — blessings all around. We're literally all connected when we yield to Love.

According to Martin Luther King Jr., "forgiveness is not just an occasional act: It is a permanent attitude."[47] Do you have a large financial debt? Give more Love. This opens your life to receiving Love. This is how the Law of Love works. Recognizing Love — sharing love, accepting love — provides whatever needs we require. Rev. Severin Simonsen spells it out further:

God, Spirit, is the only substance and supply — always at hand,
always available — the ful[l]ness of everpresent Love....

Inasmuch as the idea, money — not the material money, "the

god of this world" — embodies the essential nature, character, and quality of honesty, justice, righteousness, appreciation, etc., all being attributes of God, we rightfully conclude that the material symbol of money is emblematic of real or spiritual substance, that is, the God qualities.... man is never without substance, neither has he been, is not now, nor ever can be separated from it; for God is the omnipresent substance and supply of every needful idea to His own reflected image, man.... Furthermore, he will have a harvest — scant or abundant, good or evil — commensurate with his thinking.

Hence the importance in all our thinking is to banish from our consciousness the belief that substance and supply are in or of matter, and know and realize that it is always spiritual and eternal.[48]

I've found time and time again that when suffering from financial woes, the only way to correct the experience of lack is for me to truly accept the abundance of Love: to give gratitude for the many blessings I already have, and to find new ways to serve and love others in whatever I am called to do throughout each day. There's an insightful hymn that says: "Our gratitude is riches, complaint is poverty."[49] Watch and see. Worry breeds more lack, whereas *confidence* (literally "with trust") brings plenty. In every case, when in a financial crisis, if I turn to Love the immediate needs are met specifically in ways I couldn't possibly have imagined. This lesson was once taught to me in no uncertain terms:

Years ago I was deeply in debt, and after several major setbacks beyond my control I saw that I was unable to dig myself out. At that time there wasn't much I could do about it. In the meantime, I had discovered through my prayer and study that one of my character flaws was a *deficit* of compassion in my life: I felt unable to relate to most people, and became so aware of this that I was ashamed and intolerant of my own insensitivity, determined to correct it with God's qualities.

I worked diligently for several years, daily asking God to give me opportunities to be more compassionate and loving, to show me what real Love is. I learned this slowly but surely through relationships with friends, family, business associates and other acquaintances — how to open up more, how to give more of myself, how to really listen, etc. I was grateful to be growing spiritually.

One day out of the blue a relative whom I had grown to dearly love offered to help pay off my substantial debt, no strings attached. I was dumbfounded. With profound gratitude, I realized this immeasurable blessing was simply another indication of Love's Law in action.

Although I have not yet been able to return the favor to the same degree, I have found humbler ways to "pay it forward"[50] to the best of my ability. There are countless ways this powerful proof of God's care has been a lesson that keeps on teaching me how to love.

Do you have a problem dealing with sin in your own behavior, or in another? As Neale Donald Walsch, celebrated author of the *Conversations with God* book series advises, let's ask ourselves moment by moment: "What would Love do now?"[51]

Be loving. Receive Love. Love your neighbor *as* yourself. This is true prayer, *living* prayer. In fact, before he taught The Lord's Prayer, Jesus said that mere recitation has nothing at all to do with genuine prayer. He explained: God already "knows what you need before you ask" and then followed his prayer immediately with this sentiment: If you forgive others when they sin against you, God will also forgive you. But if you do not forgive others their sins, God will not forgive your sins (see Matthew 6:8; 14–15). In other words, self-imposed punishment is the price we pay when we turn away from Love (when we refuse to forgive).

On the other hand, ever-unfolding joy results when we choose Love. What we most need is a prayerful striving for spiritual growth, which comes from daily expressing the qualities of Love — patience, peace, good deeds, generosity, compassion, and kindness. This is the only "debt" we "owe" to Love, and the only worthwhile expression of our gratitude for what Love has done and is doing for all of us.[52] The good news is that we are *already* wholly holy! Thus Love's supply is infinite — and we will always be up to the task — with more Love to give away, and more Love to welcome in.

Love, our debt to God who gives it,
All compassion is, and kind;
Charity the law fulfilleth,
Mid the nations rancor stilleth;
Loving hearts in friendship blend,
One in [God], our heavenly Friend.[53]

LOVE

adorable

pleasing

feeling

attachment

devotion

worship

loyalty

like

yearning

sentiment

desire

tenderness

venerate

cherish

darling

sweetness

fancy

treasure

hold dear

exalt

affection

quality

fondness

regard

fidelity

emotion

ardor

passion

allegiance

piety

fervor

appreciate

beloved

honey

delight

prize

value

cuddle

reverence

favor

admire

enchantment

gift

warmhearted

benevolence

embrace

profound

consecration

esteem

friendship

bond

courtesy

generous

honor

relish

covenant

unwavering

sanctity

encourage

charming

beauty

endearment

consideration

charity

steadfast

mutual concern

enduring

connection

affinity

bountiful

kindness

nourish

applaud

constant

resolute

shelter

mercy

forgiveness

grace

THIS BLANK PAGE FOR YOUR NOTES AND PRAYERS

ENDNOTES

THE LAW OF LOVE ELIMINATES FEAR

1   See *Retrospection and Introspection*, p. 61:13–20.

2   See Gangaji public meeting.

3   *Jesus and Buddha: The Parallel Sayings*. Ed. by Marcus Borg. Berkeley, CA: Ulysses Press, 1997, p. 19. Hereinafter referred to as *Jesus and Buddha*.

4   See *S&H*, p. 454:9–13.

5   *Jesus and Buddha*, p. 15.

6   All quotes and details taken directly from the film *The Fifth Element*. Culver City, CA: Columbia Pictures/Columbia Tristar Home Video, 1997.

7   *S&H*, p. 222:21–22.

8   "Protected at Gunpoint," by Daniel Biwila. *The Christian Science Sentinel*, v. 107, no. 44, October 31, 2005, p. 12–13.

9   *Return From Tomorrow*, by George G. Ritchie with Elizabeth Sherrill. Grand Rapids, MI: Fleming H. Revell, 1978, 2001, p. 115–116. Hereinafter referred to as *Return From Tomorrow*.

10   For the full account see *Return From Tomorrow*, p. 113–116.

11   See www.worldprayers.org.

12   See *S&H*, p. 192:30–31. See also *S&H*, p. 1:1–4.

13   For more on *karuna*, see *World Religions*, p. 537.

14   See *More New Testament Words*, by William Barclay. London: SCM Press, Ltd., 1958, p. 156.

15   "Forgive and Your Health Won't Forget," by Jane Lampman. *The Christian Science Monitor*, Dec. 19, 2002, p. 11.

16   *What's So Amazing About Grace?* by Philip Yancey. Grand Rapids: Zondervan Publishing House, 1997, p. 82. Hereinafter referred to as *What's So Amazing About Grace?*

17   *What's So Amazing About Grace?*, p. 210.

18   See *S&H,* p. 476:32–477:5.

19   See *An Illustrated Encyclopaedia of Traditional Symbols* by J. C. Cooper. London/New York: Thames and Hudson, 1978, 1993, p. 117–118. Hereinafter referred to as *An Illustrated Encyclopaedia of Traditional Symbols.*

20   *S&H,* p. 266:11–12.

21   The italics are mine. Otherwise the text is intact except that I have rendered generic any references to God as "He." For the full original passage, see *No and Yes,* by Mary Baker Eddy. Boston: The Christian Science Publishing Society, 1891, 1908, p. 30:2–23.

22   See *Strong's,* p. 15 of the *New Strong's™ Concise Dictionary of the Words in the Greek Testament with Their Renderings in the King James Version* and p. 96 of the *New Strong's™ Concise Dictionary of the Words in the Hebrew Bible with Their Renderings in the King James Version.*

23   "A Spiritual Answer to Addiction," a lecture given by healer Kathleen Clemenson, Ashland Middle School, Ashland, Oregon, May 6, 2002.

24   See *The Lost Art of Forgiving: Stories of Healing From the Cancer of Bitterness* by Johann Christoph Arnold. Farmington, PA: The Plough Publishing House of The Bruderhof Foundation, 1998, p. 66 and 74.

25   See "From Barriers to Bridges," *The Christian Science Monitor,* Nov. 13, 2002, p. 23. [There is no author given.]

26   See www.ictv1.com/drums/babaolatunji. Babatunde Olatunje (1928–2003) was a Nigerian drummer who influenced many rock musicians from Mickey Hart to Carlos Santana. This quote has also been attributed to A. A. Milne.

27   *S&H,* p. 547:25–27.

28   *Matter Myth,* p. 134.

29   *Matter Myth,* p. 134.

30   *Thinking Allowed.*

31   *Thinking Allowed.*

32   *Autobiography of a Yogi,* p. 319–321.

33   For fascinating reading about the nature of time, read *A Brief History*

of Time: From the Big Bang to Black Holes by Stephen Hawking (New York: Bantam Books, 1988, rev. 1998) and a provocative work of fiction called *Einstein's Dreams* by Alan Lightman (New York: Warner Books, 1994).

34 *The Seven Spiritual Laws of Success: A Practical Guide to the Fulfillment of Your Dreams,* by Deepak Chopra. San Rafael, CA: Amber-Allen Publishing and New World Library, 1994, p. 73–74. Hereinafter referred to as *Seven Spiritual Laws of Success.*

35 See *S&H* p. 28:6–8.

36 See *S&H*, p. 254:10–15.

37 *Miscellaneous Writings*, p. 8:9–16.

38 *Miscellaneous Writings*, p. 9:9–10.

39 *Miscellaneous Writings*, p. 12:11–14 and 28–32.

40 *Seven Spiritual Laws of Success*, p. 77.

41 "Epiphanies, Then and Now." *The Christian Science Monitor*, January 7, 2002, p. 19. [No author's name is given.]

42 *The Artist's Way: A Spiritual Path to Higher Creativity* by Julia Cameron. New York: Jeremy P. Tarcher/Putnam, 1992, p. 119-120.

43 Hence the most sacred Hindu Scriptures, including the Upanishads, are called *The Vedas.*

44 *S&H*, p. 67:32.

45 "He Intended Rape," by Shirley Schwaller. *The Christian Science Sentinel*, v. 103, no. 13, March 26, 2001, p. 10.

46 *Magical Mind, Magical Body.*

47 *What's So Amazing About Grace?*, p. 137.

48 *From the Methodist Pulpit Into Christian Science and How I Demonstrated the Abundance of Substance and Supply* by Severin E. Simonsen. Fair Oaks, CA: M. Simonsen, 1928, 1960 (9th ed.), p. 189, 206–207, 214. Rev. Simonsen was a Methodist minister who left the clergy to become a healer.

49 *Christian Science Hymnal: with Seven Hymns Written by The Reverend Mary Baker Eddy, Discoverer and Founder of Christian Science*, Hymn 249 and

and 250, words by Vivian Burnett. Boston: The Christian Science Board of Directors, 1932. Hereinafter referred to as *Hymnal*.

50   The inspired idea of transforming the world through returning a favor by "paying it forward" to three people (rather than paying it back to the person who did the favor) comes from Catherine Ryan Hyde's novel (also a film starring Helen Hunt and Kevin Spacey), *Pay It Forward* (New York: Simon & Schuster, 1999).

51   From collateral materials available at The Conversations with God Foundation Center, Ashland, Oregon. For more information on the Center and its activities go to www.cwg.org.

52   See *S&H,* p. 4:3–9.

53   *Hymnal,* Hymn 178, based on the Danish of Nicolaj F. S. Grundtvig.

Completion:
wholeness; fulfillment;
unbroken unity.

SOUL

Let's be discerning.

> "I slept and dreamt that life was joy
> I awoke and saw that life was service
> I acted and behold, service was joy."
> — Rabindranath Tagore,
> Indian poet, 1861–1941

THE OUTCOME — ONE SOUL

The Implicate Order — Soul As Hologram

In the traditional sense, the word *soul*, written in lower-case letters, refers to each individual's essential quality, something that makes an individual unique. The dictionary calls the soul "the immaterial essence, animating principle, or actuating cause of an individual life," or "a person's total self"; we also might think of the soul as each individual's personality. There is a great deal of mythology and speculation surrounding what a soul might be, but in general religious terms a soul is believed to be eternal, yet somehow it's supposed to be temporarily captive within a physical body; then it is set free when the physical body dies (and presumably before birth as well), either off to some sort of heaven or hell, or to be perpetually reincarnated.

We can call into question these assumptions, since we know materiality doesn't exist, that the body is not physical but wholly spiritual, that heaven and hell are states of thought rather than actual localities, and that death is a lie. What can Soul — this mysterious "immaterial essence" or "total self" we each possess be — but Divinity Itself?

When the word Soul is capitalized, we may first think of Carl Jung's *collective unconscious* or perhaps of Ralph Waldo Emerson's *oversoul*. But their concepts describe the phenomena of common thinking (remember the snowglobe analogy), i.e., collective human thoughts — which are changeable, and which each of us can choose either to entertain or to dismiss. "[Y]ou are not your thoughts, because they come and go," says spiritual teacher Eckhart Tolle, author of *The Power of Now*. "They're all conditioned; they're all just the contents of your mind." Instead of deriving a sense of self from the contents of mortal mind, we can simply *observe the contents*; then a deeper sense of Self arises.[1]

What is the most logical in light of what we've already established is that there forever remains One Essence, the Somethingness that is Unchanging. Thus when we know that there is only One God — also called the One Mind, Principle, Spirit, Truth, Love, Life — then we know that there is only *one* "actuating" and "animating" Principle to all Being: There is One Self, One Soul.

When we relinquish all matter for Spirit — thus awakening to the simple fact that there is One Soul — this does not mean we disappear, our individuality absorbed into Deity. Rather than experiencing a loss of identity, this awareness grants each of us "a wider sphere of thought and action, a more expansive love, a higher and more permanent peace."[2] Each of us is not a *fragment* of Deity, some small corner of occasional brilliance, but instead each individual is a unique and perfect *full* declaration of Infinity, a *complete* expression of God's boundless allness. The easiest way to grasp this is to think about a hologram. Every piece of a hologram contains the whole picture — it doesn't matter how you slice it, the entire 3-D image still remains intact. This concept isn't just an intriguing metaphor. More than one physicist today believes *the universe itself* is actually a hologram, expressing what David Bohm (Albert Einstein's protégé and one of the world's most respected quantum physicists) calls "the implicate order":

> Just as every portion of a hologram contains the image of the whole, every portion of the universe enfolds the whole. This means if we knew how to access it we could find the Andromeda galaxy in the thumbnail of our left hand. We could also find Cleopatra meeting Caesar for the first time, for in principle the whole past and implications for the whole future are also enfolded in each small region of space and time. Every cell in our body enfolds the entire cosmos.[3]

Bohm explains that "the apparent separateness of consciousness and matter is an illusion"[4] and "consciousness and matter are just different aspects of the same fundamental something, a something that has its origins in the implicate order."[5] He holds that when mystics throughout the ages have reported feelings of "cosmic oneness with the universe," they are clearly describing the implicate order; Jung's idea of synchronicity is further evidence for it.[6] Brian Josephson, 1973 winner of the Nobel Prize in physics, supports the idea that Bohm's holographic model may eventually lead to the inclusion of God (as Mind) within the framework of science.[7]

According to Einstein, "The most incomprehensible thing about the universe is that it is comprehensible." His resolute search for a Grand Unification Theory (GUT, also called the Unified Field Theory or the Theory of Everything) — which would unite all the forces and matter of the universe within a single framework — was denounced by the scientific community in the 1940s and '50s during his days at Princeton University, yet nowadays the GUT is the grail still being sought by modern physicists.[8]

After our discussion of *The Fifth Element* in the chapter on the Law of Love, it's interesting to mention here that biologist Arne Wyller goes so far as to say: "Perhaps love is the fifth elementary force in [n]ature — along with gravitation, electromagnetic interaction, and weak and strong nuclear interactions — and maybe they were all united in the great fireball of the Big Bang."[9] Leading physicist Stephen Hawking, considering the origin of the universe, points out that the laws of science couldn't have been suspended at the beginning of the universe; otherwise, "might not they fail at other times also? A law is not a law if it only holds sometimes. We must try to understand the beginning of the universe on the basis of science. It may be a task beyond our powers, but we should at least make the attempt."[10] A recent cosmology put forth by Paul Steinhardt, theoretical physicist at Princeton University, is that the universe can be explained using a cyclic model. In other words, the Big Bang is simply a transition between two cycles in "an endless process of cosmological rebirth." In a few trillion years there'll be another Big Crunch and the eternal circle will continue.[11]

While the scientists continue to battle it out, I like to think that some day true scientific logic will win, and finally there will be no more contention between science and spirituality. Scientists will know what ancient wisdom and intuition have given us all along. When we hold to the premise that there can be no duality, but instead only Mind, it's easy to view a Theory of Everything as what I call One Big Coincidence. The meaning of *coincidence* is worth exploring, since the usual definition describes something that happens by accident but only seems to have some underlying connection. When I say *coincidence* I am talking about additional meanings in Webster's that include "correspondence...in nature, character, or function," "occupying the same place in space or time," and "to be in accord or agreement." In other words, when we're looking at it all from a spiritual perspective, *coincidence is actually what is happening all the time* — not just an unusual occurrence. So when we experience these moments we call *coincidences* or *synchronicities*, we are glimpsing that everpresent *coinciding* of God and man, of Mind and ideas.[12]

God's Expression — Soul's Language

"Is a candle brought out to be put under a bushel, or under a bed? and not to be set on a candlestick? There's nothing hidden that won't eventually be manifested. If anybody has ears, let them hear!" (see Mark 4:21–23)

What we're taught in school is that the five senses — sight, sound, taste, touch, and smell — are physical. But Truth is actually revealed only through *spiritual sense*, expressed in infinite ways (not just limited to five) through Soul.

Sight, for example, is not really taking place in corporeal eyes, but in

Soul — through what Mary Baker Eddy calls "spiritual discernment."[13] With eyes open or closed, waking or dreaming, can't we dream up whatever we want to see in "the mind's eye"? The following convincing message came to me a number of years ago:

I had been working prayerfully for several weeks specifically asking God for the direction "to see what is spiritually true" each day. One morning very early, I awoke realizing I had fallen asleep while reading *Science and Health*, and I'd left the bedlight on. I looked at the clock and I could see the numbers perfectly. I thought, "oh no, I've fallen asleep with my contacts in!" I got up to take them out, and lo and behold, they weren't in. I could see perfectly, everywhere I looked, without contacts! I walked all around the house, looked out the window at the landscape, and indeed I really could see everything, crisp and clear. I looked in the mirror again. My eyes were OK. I was so joyful about this, yet I still couldn't believe it. I had always had to wear glasses or contacts since I was a teenager.

I went back to bed because it was still way too early to get up. I woke up each hour for the next two hours, seeing that clock clearly, knowing I hadn't dreamed it. But soon I started to worry and became filled with doubt: "How will I possibly explain this to my family and friends? No one will believe me! What if I'm driving without glasses and all of a sudden everything goes blurry again — I'll get in an accident! How can this really be?"

As I allowed these doubts and fears to take over, by the time I finally did get out of bed another hour later, my eyes had returned to their former blurriness!

Nevertheless, I am still especially grateful for this experience. I know that I was healed then of my nearsightedness, and that it was only the fact that I allowed doubt and fear to cloud my thinking that I let this healing slip away.

But the great thing is, about a year later, I went to the eye doctor for a check-up. He was astonished to discover that my eyesight had improved ("It's so unusual at your age" he observed) — so much so, that the astigmatism I'd had in one eye for the last 25 years was gone!

Even though I still wear glasses today, all this has taught me that our experience is indeed mental, and that some day — it could be at any moment — I will be able to claim the permanency of this healing. As God's child I can always clearly see what is spiritually true.

Just before he fed over five thousand people with only a few loaves of bread and some fishes, Jesus admonished the disciples, "Having eyes, see ye not? and having ears, hear ye not? and do ye not remember?" (Mark 8:18) Spiritual understanding is the true hearing of what Soul knows, not originating in physical ears.[14] We can listen to Truth any time, and this hearing has nothing to do with a corporeal auditory apparatus. The following account tells of a healing of tinnitus:

Every time I heard that annoying ringing, I told it off. This meant that each night, as I was trying to sleep, instead of imagining how I would live unable to hear, I used my sleeplessness as an opportunity to listen to God and what [God] was telling me. I knew that God loved me and was there with me. To me, God is all-Love, all peace, all assurance and harmony. I knew that harmony was with me. The discordant sound I was hearing was merely physical — it didn't have any spiritual origin. But God is also Spirit, so my own origin is spiritual. I was comforted by my eternal connection to God.

I did lots of studying during this period of several months with passages about hearing and ears, indeed all the senses, in *Science and Health*. I learned from this study that the physical senses are not the last word on me. They are symbols of spiritual sense. That spiritual sense is intact no matter what my physical hearing was telling me. And I have the spiritual sense that allows me to hear God. And this is all that I can hear, since [God] is all. I prayed deeply with these concepts, and my fear began to decrease. This frame of mind strengthened me, and, I think, readied me for the understanding I needed to solve the problem.

One night I had a dream. I was listening to a plaintive and moody song — *Knights in White Satin* by the Moody Blues, in fact. Although I love that song, in the dream, I said to myself, "I don't want to hear this song right now. I want something happier." And I began thinking about a hymn I knew....

When I awoke, I remembered all this clearly. And then it struck me. I had been *hearing* in my dream, and I had changed what I was hearing by my own choice. Also, in the dream, my hearing was completely unrelated to my physical ears. If I could hear in the dream without my ears, what did that imply about hearing in my waking life?

In that moment, I understood so solidly that what I hear is not a physical function at all. My ears, physical as they are, are a *symbol* of hearing, but they aren't the capacity itself. Since I have an essentially spiritual nature, given to me by God, Spirit, then I have a natural and constant capacity to hear anything [God] wants me to hear.

Wow! This new line of thought got rid of the fear once and for all. From then on, every time the ringing came, I clobbered it with that truth. And then I would rejoice in whatever other spiritual truth I had recently been contemplating, "hearing" in an entirely spiritual way. Invariably, the annoying sound would subside. Eventually it tried one last trick — it switched ears! But all I did was laugh.

Within a few months, the condition was no longer bothering me. And some time later, I realized I hadn't heard it, even in my quietest moments, for a long time. Today, several years later, my hearing is as good as ever.[15]

The One Soul not only gives each of us our individual faculties, but Soul is also the Origin of our creativity, invention, innovation, and improvisation. (Why do you think they call it "soul music"?) Certainly "the sixth sense" (extrasensory perception, or ESP) is included in Soul as well — as the epitome of intuition and spiritual insight. Many of us have had an experience of telepathy, precognition, remarkable creativity, prophetic dreaming, etc. Dr. Larry Dossey says this is because "the mind is acting at a distance from the brain and body, and often outside the present moment."[16] To me Dossey's observation points to the deeper reality: the certainty that there is One Mind, One Soul, and that distant healing through scientific prayer is simply evidence of Divine Law in action.

Soul's language is the continual unfoldment of progress — moving away from mistaken materiality to fully awaken to consummate spirituality. Soul's language is universal, transcending all tongues, cultures, time, and space. And Soul is forever speaking. There was never a moment when Soul was not expressed, nor will there ever be a time when Soul is not eloquent.

When the reality of Soul's oneness sinks in, we are liberated — free to be ourselves. If you are searching for your purpose, your career, your calling here on this planet, call up the faculties of Soul: All your skills are tapped and developed here. The potential is endless and always unfolding, which means you won't ever have to settle for being stuck in a position unsuited to you. Tuning in to Soul opens the way to freedom.

When we know we have something unique to contribute to humanity, Soul will guide us to the best way to combine our unique God-given talents and gifts with service to others. Soul's messages come to each of us personally. For instance, our prayerful intuition directs us to see signs everywhere: We might hear a conversation that changes everything, pick up a newspaper article that gives us a nugget of truth, suddenly comprehend a song lyric spiritually for the first time, or discern the significance of a vivid dream.

When my daughter was first born, as a new mother I was a stressed-out businesswoman seriously reevaluating my career path. I hadn't really had a chance yet to write this book in earnest, although I was making the attempt. During that time:

> I had a dream that I possessed a big magical book. It would tell me great truths: Extraordinary words would come off of the paper and light up in 3-D, and dance around, soon answering all kinds of clues which the book had given earlier. This went on, time after time, each problem being answered by this book.

> Then the last one I got before waking up was only a clue — without the answer: The letters came out and danced around, all lit up, beautiful and colorful. Out came the letter *b*, and it got swallowed up by a fish — captioned with the number *1979*. Well, it made very little sense, but the dream was so vivid, I scribbled it down on a scrap of paper.

> A couple of days later I saw that slip of paper, and I thought: "Oh! '*Be* swallowed by a fish'! — I get it! Jonah!" So I reread the biblical story of Jonah, discovering all sorts of new ideas. Soon I was obliged to take a detour to a bookstore, because I saw the billboard "*Providence* Occupational Center" — it was all just too obvious to me. There I found commentary, etc. on Jonah (the first rack I looked at).

> Just for fun I decided to look up the number *1979* in both dictionaries in my *Strong's Bible Concordance*: it's *haliykah*, the Hebrew word for "walking," "step," "way," or "going"; as well as the Greek word *episitismos* derived from the word *epi* for "toward" or "rest upon" plus *sitos* meaning "provision," "victuals," or "grain" (I immediately revisited the biblical story of the tares and the wheat).

> As I learned more and grew spiritually, I continued exploring

the Jonah story on various levels. The problem of Jonah's *righteous anger* was helpful — something I had been specifically working to eliminate in myself at the time. There was also the fact that *Jonah* means "dove," which symbolizes peace and forgiveness.

Over a year later I also realized that a fish symbolizes The Christ Consciousness.[17] Eventually I woke up to ask myself: Was I headed for Tarshish instead of Ninevah?[18] It soon became easier and easier to answer the calling to finish writing this book. My spiritual work on these ideas is still ongoing.

Not only that — during that stage of my life I had been struggling with a severe case of eczema on my hands. Eczema, an irritating skin condition which literally means "to boil" and "yeast," includes inflammation and itching. Of course it was no surprise that some of the issues I'd been prayerfully working to reject in my experience at that time were annoyance, exasperation, and anger. As I allowed the *leaven* of these ideas to work in my heart, the many aspects of anger that had been affecting me so deeply were overcome one by one — replaced with such Divine qualities as forbearance, patience, calm, solace, comfort, and peace. (I could fill another book with the lessons I learned during this time!) Holding steadfastly to each spiritual truth I learned, after a long struggle the eczema was gone.

When we stay open to the messages of Soul, knowing Life is all One Big Coincidence, instances of serendipity will increasingly fill the moments of our days, bringing joy and healing to all our activities.

Soul, God, is sinless, perfect, never enclosed in a material body. Soul is immaterial and immortal, Soul is Spirit (both impossible to render in the plural), and without location, boundary, or physicality.[19] When we know the outcome in every circumstance is One Soul, we know salvation is universal. Salvation is actually a liberated state of consciousness. As One Soul forever expressed, we are all connected, and blended in harmony. There are not many souls, some blessed and others accursed to damnation. As mentioned earlier in the chapter of the Law of Life, we know that people can never dwell in hell of any sort except one of their own making. Heaven is ever-present.

Our goal as spiritual beings, then, is not to "save souls" but to liberate Soul in each individual. Since there are no separate souls to save, and God is All Good, it's our responsibility to awaken to the reality of Soul. When fully awake, we see there is no condemnation. We are safe ("saved") and sound in the arms of Infinite Soul. We can't ever lose our abilities, talents, purpose, or direction, because it's in our very nature to express Soul. Then we can heal, and help others to heal.

Progress Is The Law Of God

"[P]rogress is the law of God, whose law demands of us only
what we can certainly fulfill." — Mary Baker Eddy[20]

It is our human experience that everything is always in motion. Change is the only constant. Let's look at this idea first as is, and then turn it upside-down.

First of all, when times are tough, it's often difficult to see our way out. We can easily feel hopeless, confused, and overwhelmed. Years later, when a bad time is long past, however, we are able to see the headway we've made. Most of the time we can even acknowledge blessings that came from a tragedy, or see a good reason for a particular event, when at the time the circumstances appeared to be random chaos and heartache. In the course of what we call our human lives, we go from point A to B to C, and there may be millions of ways to get there. We may think we're taking sideroads or back alleys that don't make sense at the time; but eventually, looking with hindsight at the big picture, we can discern an Intelligence in motion, making sense behind it all. (Remember our discussion about "the wisdom of uncertainty" in the chapter on the Law of Life.) Trusting in the direction of Life is the way to know for certain that God's Law always means progress — and it can't ever be stopped. What we perceive as setbacks (either in our personal lives, in society, or worldwide) are just steps along the way in the infinite unfolding advancement of progress.

Did you know that mathematicians have been unable to prove the principle of randomness?[21] David Bohm, explaining further the implicate order of the universe, says "maybe things that we perceive as disordered aren't disordered at all.... they only appear to us as random" in the same way a hologram seems disordered to the naked eye — just interference patterns on a piece of film. The order is simply "hidden or *enfolded*" within. In other words, our everyday lives are really an illusion, like a holographic image. Yet underlying is "a deeper order of existence.... [While] Bohm calls this deeper level of reality the *implicate* ('enfolded') order, he refers to our own level of existence as the *explicate*, or unfolded, order."[22]

Now let's go back and restate the same idea — "change is the only constant" — from another angle: Nothing ever stays the same. That's right: The nature of Nothing is that it is always the same. In other words, Nothing (evil) is always in flux, always moving, always unpredictable! However, we know that Nothing's constant chaos — materiality — isn't what's really going on. Nothing is still exactly *what isn't.*

The Apostle Paul advises: "Be sober, be vigilant; because your adversary, the devil, as a roaring lion, walketh about, seeking whom he may devour" (I Peter 5:8). The devil, in other words, is always trying to stir things up, in order to instill fear and doubt so that we'll be distracted from the Truth. Spiritual teacher Gangaji reminds us that although we're perpetually "fascinated by what moves" — that is, captivated by the drama that life is when we view it as mortal and material — whenever we're faced with any sort of challenge, instead of focusing on the problems and trying to fix them, we simply need to stop. We can choose to be vigilant in our thinking. Then we recognize that God is unmoving. As Gangaji puts it, when we understand this fact we can see that "we are Vigilance Itself."[23] Like the still waters of a lake we can then perfectly reflect the reality of The One (see the chapter on the Law of Truth). The underlying reality of Life doesn't ever change. In this spiritual sense, Life is unmoving, solid, profound, all-known, and complete. This is our home. This is where Soul dwells.

While we know that God is "unmoving," we also know that everything is "in motion" at all times and in all places in the universe — from atomic particles to our planet and beyond. This fact means that we must remain vigilant, but vigilance doesn't mean rigidity; on the contrary, scientific prayer requires complete openness to Truth at all times. This spiritualization of thought comes moment by moment: When we express this diligent watchfulness, we must always be ready to make a radical shift if necessary. And whatever changes we need to make, we don't have to go it alone. Remember, it's impossible to be alone. Our God, The "All-One," leads the way for us. Bohm explains this delightful paradox scientifically. Einstein, Bohm's mentor, established that space and time aren't separate but part of a larger whole called the spacetime continuum. Bohm adds:

> [E]verything in the universe is part of a continuum. Despite the apparent separateness at the explicate level, everything is a seamless extension of everything else.... Look at your hand. Now look at the light streaming from the lamp.... You are not merely made of the same things. *You are the same thing....* this does not mean the universe is a giant undifferentiated mass. Things can be part of an undivided whole and still possess their own unique qualities.[24]

Like individual eddies and currents, each of us is part of the vast ocean of Soul's Consciousness.

Give Up

> "Since everyone has received the gift, even so, minister the
> same to each other, as good defenders of the manifold grace
> of God." (see I Peter 4:10)

Whenever we awaken to spiritual reality, we can give up at last. What does it mean to give up? *Give up* your own will and your life, and turn it all over to God — i.e., yield your whole self to Good, to Love, to Life! But not only that. It doesn't mean you're losing out on anything! It doesn't mean you've failed. It doesn't mean you're killing yourself — either literally or metaphorically. It means you've learned that basing one's life on a material sense of things will always be disappointing.

But learning this fact doesn't mean we have to live in deprivation in order to be "enlightened." Giving up is *not* a defeat. It's victory! It's finally opening ourselves up to Life's never-ending and overflowing abundance.

"Must I give up my business and go into a monastery?" a man once asked a Holy One, so an ancient story goes. The answer came: "Oh, no, no, never. I am saying, hold on to your business but go into your heart."[25]

Edward Kimball (1845–1909), a student of Mary Baker Eddy's in Chicago who devoted his life to spiritual healing and later became a respected teacher and lecturer,

> was so enthusiastic when he saw what could be accomplished
> through a clear understanding and faithful appliance of its
> Principle, that he wrote to Mrs. Eddy how deeply grateful he was
> for Christian Science, and added, that he was willing to give up
> everything for Science. Mrs. Eddy did not stop to write a letter
> and send her message by mail, but she wired him and said, "Dear
> Student: you do not have to give up anything except error."
>
> What we need to give up is our false belief of life, health,
> strength, pleasure, pain and substance in matter. It means to
> come out and *be ye separate,* [see II Corinthians 6:17] and give up
> looking upon, holding to, and leaning upon matter as a reality
> — as substance.[26]

This type of faith is born from an understanding heart, in which we can learn and then teach others how to recognize God's perfect man — never to worship or fear a manmade God.[27] The Apostle Paul's admonition to come out of the world and "be ye separate" doesn't mean hiding from the problems of the world. A "flight from the world" isn't about leaving a particular location. It's about shedding one set of attitudes, one kind of consciousness for another.[28]

Once we give up the error of materiality and embrace the Truth of spirituality, "giving up" then also takes on another new meaning. Giving *up* can mean serving others: By viewing all people in a spiritual light — not in the mistaken view of material judgment — we can lift everyone *up* out of the confusion of mortal existence to the peace and purpose of Soul's perfect interconnectedness. Start giving. Keep giving. Give more and more to those in need. Marilyn Puder-York, whose Battery Park City home office survived just south of the World Trade Center collapse, defines "soul" as a shift in values from "the pursuit of money to a balanced caring and compassionate empathy for others while in the pursuit of excellence.... It's time to get rid of the selfish, narcissistic, bottom-line-only mentality."[29] This ought not to be just wishful thinking. The time to act is now. Indeed, physicist David Bohm goes so far as to say that humanity's seemingly universal tendency to fragment the world, to ignore our dynamic interconnectedness, is behind most of the world's problems — both personal and global — and "may even lead to our extinction."[30]

We can start today to give *up*. When we give up a mistaken material view and adopt a spiritual view, we can truly start to give — to ourselves, to our spouse, to our friends, to our children, to our grandchildren, to our parents, to our neighbors, to strangers, to *enemies*, to *anybody* — we are *giving* so as to bring people *up* to the realization of the Truth: that God is ever-present Love, Life, and Harmony.

We can decide to bring everyone up, not down. Meet a need. And watch. And see.

Situations will improve everywhere you look, everywhere you go, in everything you do. You have to start somewhere. Open a door for the delivery guy loaded down with packages. Hand a purse to a woman who's almost forgotten it in her cart at the grocery store parking lot. Smile at that bored bank teller. Buoy them *up!* Give some more, in these little ways, and in big ways too — lend a hand during a crisis, share a laugh in a moment of sadness, etc. Just be sure to always give *up*.

When this spiritual perspective becomes our way of life, we cannot lack. We can never be down while we're giving *up*. This is the start of learning and living an "unselfed love" (as discussed in the chapter on the Law of Love), of sharing the complete freedom of nondual realization with the world. "Unselfed," we can surrender the ego completely, and when this happens we'll no longer be afraid of anything, because we'll see we're living in the One Self, reflecting the One Soul. This is where permanent healing takes place.

Spiritual teacher Andrew Cohen tells us that "the goal now, as audacious as it sounds, is not merely to transcend the world, but to transform the world, to become an agent of the evolutionary impulse itself. Indeed, in surrendering one's ego to *that*, one literally feels oneself being filled up with a divine and luminous energy and a passion to transform the world and the whole universe for a cause that has nothing to do with oneself."[31] According to psychologist Lawrence LeShan, who has conducted many studies on the subject of spiritual healing, spiritual healers in general possess an attitude of selflessness, of *being* instead of *doing*: "One can only be fully in this mode when one has, if only for a moment, given up all wishes and desires for oneself (since the separate self does not exist) and for others (since they do not exist as separate either) and just allow oneself to be and therefore to be with and be one with the [A]ll of existence."[32]

As honest seekers for Truth,[33] it is our purpose each day to be open to what God knows, and thus to serve all people in every action we take, grand or mundane. We don't serve merely out of a sense of duty, but more importantly because unselfed Love teaches us that we must serve by virtue of our very nature. The Apostle Paul explains Jesus' most powerful teaching: "For all the law is fulfilled in one word, even in this; Thou shalt love thy neighbor as thyself" (Galatians 5:12). When we take Jesus' directive to heart, we can see the presence of God everywhere, in spite of how inconceivable the circumstances may be. Equipped with our understanding of the Allness of Divine Power — what Paul called "the whole armour of God" (see Ephesians 6:10-18) — each of us possesses what it takes to remain sane in an insane world, the security of which depends on an open heart. Desert monastic Abba Benjamin echoed the words of Paul when he advised: "Do this and you will be saved: Rejoice always, pray constantly, and in all circumstances give thanks" (see I Thessalonians 5:16–18).[34] When we rejoice — with genuine joy, praise and gratitude — "it is not the joy of fools.... It is not the praise of the ingratiating," says Benedictine Sister Joan Chittister. She continues:

> The contemplative knows struggle when difficulties come. It is not the gratitude of the obtuse. The contemplative recognizes the difference between chaff and grain. The contemplative knows that grain is for bread, but the contemplative also knows that chaff is for heat. [Recall our discussion of the tares and the wheat in the chapter on the Law of Truth.] The contemplative realizes that everything in life has for its purpose the kindling of the God-life within us. And so the contemplative goes on with joy and resounds with praise and lives in gratitude. Always. What better way to bring the light of the diamond to glow in the darkness.[35]

Go On

> "We must accept finite disappointment, but we must never lose infinite hope." — Martin Luther King, Jr.

So often we hear the expression "life goes on." When you've been through a time of failure, loss, or grief, you have to pick yourself up and go on. OK, easier said than done. So what does it really mean, *to go on*? Should you doggedly live the way you've been living? Keep doing things the way you've been doing them? No, obviously that's not going to work very well. But how can you go on the same way, when you've experienced such profound heartbreak?

You must move forward, but somehow you must also *grow*. And the only way to do that is to go *on*, not *off*! So go forward with your light on, not off, and you will prosper, you will heal, you will grow, you will regain your joy. The Light is still shining. It never stops. Pick it up, turn it on — use this flashlight to illuminate your new path. God has the batteries, and they never run out of juice!

When we admit that God is in control, has always been in control, will always be in control, we allow our lives to blossom and grow in ways we could never have imagined. So let's allow Mind to think, Principle to rule, Spirit to soar, Truth to be told, Life to thrive, Love to comfort, and Soul to sing.

The fundamental paradox of each person's individuality — which simultaneously exists completely intact and interconnected within the One Self — was brought home to me one evening when our family sat down to dinner. We sang the blessing before the meal as we often do, and our daughter, four years old at the time, asked about why we changed notes. She was accustomed to hearing the tune in unison, but my husband and I had thrown in some harmonizing for the "Amen." As we explained the concept of harmony to her, my husband told her "each singer has to stick to their own note — then we have harmony." To fully express all the wonderful qualities of God, each of us must express God in our own *unique* individual way. This is the only way the One Soul can exist! Let's celebrate diversity — it's absolutely vital to our survival because it's one of the best ways there is to support each other's gifts, thereby illuminating the universal awareness of God's very expression.

Follow the way God calls you and guides you, and jump out there on the path ahead with both feet — no reason to be bashful or fearful. With this act of courage, we can embrace our divine childhood, knowing our individual purpose and destiny are safe in God's hands for all time. And on our journey let's cheer every brother and sister alongside. A common Nepali greeting or farewell is the Sanskrit word *namasté*, whose original intent can be rendered as "I honor the Divine within you." Hands are pressed together in prayer position, drawn from the forehead to the heart, with the head slightly bowed. *Namasté* and *thanks* are two of the most powerful words we can live today. Let's honor that infinite place that embodies each of us — created, constituted and governed by Love, Truth, Peace, and Light.[36]

By Grace Are We Saved

"For by grace are you saved through faith; it is not of
yourselves, it is the gift of God." (see Ephesians 2:8)

The importance of grace in our ability to see spiritually cannot be underestimated. Grace — the idea of *unconditional* love — is perhaps one of the most difficult concepts for us to grasp. The story of Jesus' ultimate sacrifice on the cross "for our sins" seems incalculable, and certainly beyond what any of us deserve. Yet the implications are profound. When Jesus showed us that materiality and death aren't real, he liberated us from the lie of sin, making us free to embrace the Truth of Love. This is the revelation of grace that Jesus imparted — with the power to transform. The word *grace* means "unmerited divine assistance given humans for their regeneration or sanctification," and "a virtue coming from God"; as well as "mercy," "pardon," "privilege," or "reprieve." We can't earn God's approval by our own efforts; we must receive it as a gift, with arms wide open.[37] As C. S. Lewis says about grace, "A man whose hands are full of parcels can't receive a gift."[38]

Grace used as a verb means "to confer dignity or honor on," "adorn," or "embellish." How do we bring ourselves to accept this unearned gift of honor? Really, the only way is to do so without judgment or reservation — with gratitude. *Grace* in fact comes from the Latin *gratia* meaning "thanks" or "favor," from *gratus*, meaning "pleasing" or "grateful." The word for *grace* in Greek, *kharis*, is part of the word *eukharista*, meaning "gratitude"; *eukharistos* means "grateful." Consequently grace is "the quality or state of being considerate or thoughtful." Accepting God's grace *is* therefore expressing gratitude. When Paul says "by grace are you saved" he wasn't talking only about the redemption of Jesus' death and resurrection. His words also convey the idea that *gratitude is what makes us whole*. The word *saved* means "preserved from danger or harm," "protected," and "safe." The origin of *safe* goes back to the Latin word *salvus*, meaning "healthy," akin to *solidus* ("solid") and to the Greek *holos* ("whole") and the Sanskrit *sarva* ("entire"). In plain English, gratitude is good for you! A *Christian Science Monitor* article spells out the effectiveness of gratitude:

Thanking God isn't a way to manipulate God so I can get what I want. It's not like eating my vegetables so that I can be rewarded with dessert. But being willing to recognize the good that God is giving me is a powerful way to feel closer to [God]. And when I feel closer to [God], I naturally find more harmony, joy, freedom, love — more healing....

God is constantly giving each of [God's] children love, joy, peace, freedom, strength....

One time I was very ill and wasn't feeling that divine love and presence. I was relying on God to bring an end to intense pain. But not finding any relief, I asked a friend to read to me from the book of Psalms in the Bible. I'll never forget the powerful effect these psalms had. The pain dissolved almost immediately as I agreed with the power and presence of God in the Psalmist's life as well as in my own.[39]

Whatever we don't nourish within ourselves can't exist in the world around us because we are its microcosm.[40] We can always ask God each moment for guidance and forgiveness, and give thanks for every glimpse of beauty in our lives. The opportunity to spiritualize experience begins here.

Once you get into practice, the good things to be grateful for will flow minute by minute throughout the day. If you have trouble expressing gratitude at first, keep a Gratitude Notebook (I call mine my "Good Things/ Good Thinks Book"). Write a letter to yourself and watch it become a prayer of thanksgiving: Fill your heart with Soul's Love. Every morning write down what you are thankful for. Every night write down what you are thankful for. Make yourself do it — no matter how long it takes for you to recall something good. Something else I do is to write thank-you notes to people. I keep a running list of people who have given me something or done something for which I am grateful. Every few days or so I sit down and write them notes of gratitude. How special it is to send and receive such a card in the mail — to be reminded of our simple gifts. Over time these expressions of gratitude become easier, until there will be too many good things to count. Then the thankfulness becomes an automatic response. This attitude of gratitude makes us healthier. And we'll find ourselves turning to God in gratitude even in — especially in — times of crisis.

Celebrated poet Maya Angelou tells about a time in the early 1950s when she had returned to America leaving a child behind in Europe. Frightened for her very sanity, she went to her voice teacher for solace. He told her to pick up a yellow pad and write down her blessings. Although she resisted, he told her to start with the fact that she could hear him, that she could see the page, that she was capable of holding the pen. "Before I reached the end of the page," she recounts, "I was transformed." Ever since, she has written everything on a yellow pad. "As soon as I pick it up, I am reminded of my blessings."[41]

To cultivate the attitude of gratitude in our families, we can teach our children to get in the habit of listing things they're thankful for. This can be called "The Glad Game."[42] Sitting around the dinner table, each person can say what makes him or her glad on that particular day. I have often found that the gratitude itself *is* the healing. When my daughter has fallen down and hurt herself, when she's throwing a tantrum, or when she can't get to sleep, I tell her to stop crying or complaining — and start right now to give thanks: "Remember who you are. You are God's child. And you are all right. Say your prayers, and tell our Father-Mother God what you're thankful for." Once she gets started counting her blessings, she keeps going, and invariably forgets all about what was bothering her. As grownups we can do this too. This gear-switching to the spiritual reality is an easy and joyful way to kick Satan's "…but…"! (See the chapter on Truth.)

Christ Jesus was certainly in the habit of giving thanks. Even when facing the death of his friend Lazarus, he started out his prayer with gratitude: "Father, I thank You that You have heard me, and I know that You always hear me; but because of the people which stand by I say it, that they may believe that You have sent me." Even though Lazarus had been dead four days already, Jesus wasn't discouraged. He simply cried with a loud voice, "Lazarus, come forth" and Lazarus emerged from the tomb alive.[43]

Each of us is a reflection of Allness — think about how vast and marvelous that is. The One Soul is Infinite! Overflowing Love, healing, and joy. We are here to heal and grow, not to wallow in the mire of material unreality. *God* doesn't believe the lies about materiality that we so often tell each other; in fact, God doesn't even *know* about them. God is forever telling us only the truth about the perfection of spiritual reality.

Divinity emanates only happiness and harmony. So that's what we naturally reflect and project. Our unique gifts and talents have been given by God and are indestructible. There are so many reasons to be grateful. It's our responsibility and privilege to go out there every day and share these blessings with others.

The Most Polished Stone

"The whole of creation is perfect. There is a natural law that operates on this planet and in the universe. Everything works in a perfect order. There's a scheme to all things that has a certain intelligence, that drives everything. But it requires that we, as individuals, go to that level of consciousness and bring it into our being. If we could have people who are conscious, in a spiritual sense, all the underlying problems in society would change." — George Harrison[44]

We don't make Truth happen. Our job is simply to *bear witness* to Truth's constant authority and activity.[45] To the degree that we do this, we will better our experience. Scientific prayer doesn't change or correct reality — it *reveals* reality. It is a matter of discovery for each of us.[46]

Right at this very moment, you have the courage and the resources to conquer the Goliath you must face, even against all odds. The courage you need will come from the realization that the Divine is in you, that you express Divine Power, and that therefore nothing within the grasp of your understanding is too distant for the grasp of your hand.[47]

The Hebrew word for "smooth" in the David and Goliath story is *khalook*, from the word *khalak*, used for the smooth stones employed in those times for drawing lots; thus *khalak* and words related to it are sometimes applied in the Bible for the English word "portion," or "lot." The smoothest stone tells each of us irrefutably that our birthright as God's child is secured. Our destiny is already known — our lot in life can be only good! Now, you can reach out to God and choose your five smooth stones, with confidence and with joy, knowing every step of the way your victory is sure.

Each of us on life's journey comes to cherish at least one truth — one spiritual fact that is true for us deep down in our hearts because we've proven it for ourselves without any doubt. It's one truth we grow to discern without effort, and with absolute certainty. It's the one "stone in our bag" that's "the most polished" because of our constant handling of it, since we know it so well and have applied it successfully so many times. And just as David found out, *one smooth stone* is really all we need — no armor, slogans, affirmations, complex arguments, or analyses are necessary. In a crisis, the smoothest stone will do. Even in those times when we endure a prolonged challenge, ultimately, it takes only one good idea to bring healing.

SOUL

SPIRIT

heart

animated

LIFE

being

vitality

immortality

existence

character

quintessence

substance

wight (Icelandic: being, creature;
          brave, strong)
nonsensuous

TRUTH

introspection

contemplation

thought

sentiment

quality

sea ("habitation of the soul")

MIND

essence

PRINCIPLE

living

élan

breath

permanent individual

conscience

pith

virtuality

individuality

noumenon

radiance

strong

breast

bosom

reflection

action

feeling

anima

courageous/brave

music!

source

resources

stuff

see

hear

taste/savor

smell/fragrance

faculty

intuition

rhythm

color

infinity

eloquence

freedom

joy

wholeness

intact

melody

core

LOVE

searching

guts

artistry

talent

creativity

grandeur

beauty

distinctiveness

spontaneity

symmetry/balance

calm

wit

grace

poise

tranquillity

merriment

original

improvisation

activity

THIS BLANK PAGE FOR YOUR NOTES AND PRAYERS

ENDNOTES

THE OUTCOME — ONE SOUL

1   "Beyond Happiness and Unhappiness: An Interview with Spiritual Teacher Eckhart Tolle," by Steven Donoso. *The Sun*, issue 319, July 2002, p. 9.

2   *S&H*, p. 265:10–15.

3   *Holographic Universe*, p. 50.

4   *Holographic Universe*, p. 79.

5   *Holographic Universe*, p. 133.

6   *Holographic Universe*, p. 63, 79.

7   *Holographic Universe*, p. 54.

8   "Who Knew? Try Einstein," by Gregory M. Lamb. *The Christian Science Monitor*, November 14, 2002, p. 15.

9   *Planetary Mind*, p. 240–241.

10   *The Universe in a Nutshell* by Stephen W. Hawking. New York: Bantam Books, 2001, p. 79.

11   "Universe Reborn Endlessly in New Model of the Cosmos," by Ben Harder. *National Geographic News*, April 25, 2002. At www.nationalgeographic.com.

12   See also *S&H*, p. 193:32 and p. 561:16.

13   See "Eyes" in the Glossary section of *S&H*, p. 586:3–6.

14   See "Ears" in the Glossary section of *S&H*, p. 585:1–4.

15   Blog posting on the Website of my friend, healer Laura Matthews, April 27, 2005. Visit her blog at www.lbmatthews.com.

16   *Reinventing Medicine*, p. 10.

17   Early Christians started using the symbol of a fish as a secret rebus code to identify themselves. The Greek word for *fish* is *ichthus*: *Iesous Christos Theou Huios Soter* (Jesus Christ, Son of God, Saviour). See *An*

Illustrated Encyclopaedia of Traditional Symbols, p. 68.

18   As the story goes, God calls Jonah to preach to the people of Ninevah, but Jonah goes the other way, on a boat headed for Tarshish. He is thrown overboard and swallowed by "a great fish" and stays in its belly for three days before he prays and is then tossed up on the shore. For the whole tale see the Book of Jonah in the Old Testament of the Bible.

19   See Mary Baker Eddy's answers to the following questions in *S&H*: "What are spirits and souls?" p. 466:7–31, and "What are body and Soul?" p. 477:19–478:13. Also see p. 482:3–12.

20   *S&H,* p. 233:6–7.

21   *Holographic Universe,* p. 44.

22   See *Holographic Universe,* p. 44, 46.

23   "Vigilance."

24   *Holographic Universe,* p. 48. Italics in the original.

25   *The Monastic Way: Walking Through Life Whole and Holy,* a monthly newsletter from Joan Chittister. Erie, PA: Benetvision, April 2002.

26   *From the Methodist Pulpit Into Christian Science,* p. 220–221.

27   In the video "Mary Baker Eddy: Daughter of New England...Citizen of the World..." presented by The Mary Baker Eddy Library for the Betterment of Humanity™ and The First Church of Christ, Scientist in Boston, 2000, the motto stating the purpose of Christian Science Sunday School is as follows: "To teach how to recognize God's man, not to worship or fear a manmade God."

28   *Illuminated Life,* p. 80.

29   "A New York State of Mind," *The Christian Science Monitor,* Special Report, Sept. 28, 2001, by Alexandra Marks, Staff Writer, with Staff Writers Ron Scherer and Liz Marlantes and contributor Harry Bruinius, p. 1+.

30   *Holographic Universe,* p. 49.

31   "The Guru and the Pandit: Andrew Cohen & Ken Wilber in Dialogue — The Evolution of Enlightenment," by Andrew Cohen. *What Is Enlightenment?,* Spring/Summer 2002, p. 41. The magazine's founder, Cohen,

leads spiritual retreats throughout the world; the International Fellowship for the Realization of Impersonal Enlightenment, headquartered in Lenox, MA, is dedicated to his teachings.

32   "What is Healing?" by Larry Dossey. *Unity Magazine*, Jan./Feb. 2003, v. 183, no. 1, p. 24.

33   See *S&H*, p. xii:26.

34   *Illuminated Life*, p. 129, 141–142.

35   *Illuminated Life*, p. 142.

36   See *S&H*, p. 316:20–21.

37   See *What's So Amazing About Grace?*, p. 210.

38   *What's So Amazing About Grace?*, p. 180.

39   "Gratitude Heals," *The Christian Science Monitor*, December 13, 2002, p. 23. [No author's name is given.] Hereinafter referred to as "Gratitude Heals."

40   *Illuminated Life*, p. 29.

41   "Gratitude Heals."

42   I thank healer Julie A. Ward for sharing her ideas about playing "The Glad Game." Hayley Mills played this game as the title character in *Pollyanna*, a Disney film based on the Pollyanna stories by Eleanor Hodgman Porter.

43   For the full account see John 11:1–44 (specifically verses 41–44).

44   From a George Harrison television interview on VH-1 in 1997; quoted in *What is Enlightenment? Extra*, Winter 2002, p. 18.

45   See "Remembrance of Good — A Healing Light," by Beulah M. Roegge. *The Christian Science Journal*, v. 118, no. 3, March 2000, p. 21.

46   See "Excerpts From a Talk Given at Arden Wood on the Subject of Terrorism," by healer Jack Edward Hubbell, Feb. 21, 2002. San Francisco: Arden Wood, 2002.

47   See *Jewish Science and Health: the Textbook of Jewish Science* by Rabbi Morris Lichtenstein. Plainview, NY: The Society of Jewish Science, 1925, 1970, p. 159.

NAMASTÉ AND THANKS

"The material human concept grew beautifully less as I floated into more spiritual latitudes and purer realms of thought."
— Mary Baker Eddy

I wrote this book because I want to share the fact that prayer, when understood and practiced scientifically, is not a last resort reserved for crises when all else fails. Scientific prayer heals. And you can prove it for yourself.

I first found this out for myself in Chicago in 1991, when I was healed in a matter of days of a long-standing physical problem after reading Mary Baker Eddy's *Science and Health: with Key to the Scriptures*. Simply by reading this book, I was able to see clearly that I did not need medical care to become healthy again. Excited about what I had learned from Eddy's book, I took a stand and threw away all my medicines and herbal remedies, and decided not to go back to the chiropractor I'd been seeing on a weekly basis. I even threw away all vitamins, aspirin, and every other medicine I had in my apartment. Within a week I was completely well. Gradually over the next few years allergies and other physical problems I'd had for most of my life faded away into nothing.

A few years later I had moved to Los Angeles. It was 1992. One day out of curiosity I walked into a Christian Science Reading Room in Studio City. I wasn't sure what a Reading Room was, although I knew about the Pulitzer prize–winning *Christian Science Monitor* newspaper, and knew Eddy's writings were sold there. (I had actually found my first copy of *Science and Health* at the Evanston Public Library a few blocks from where I worked just north of Chicago. My dear friend Rebecca Fritz, to whom I will forever be grateful for suggesting I read Eddy's work, had since given me my own paperback copy, which by that time had become the most treasured and well-worn book I've ever owned. And kudos to my husband David for rescuing it from our collapsed apartment the morning of the 1994 Northridge earthquake.)

Standing there in that Reading Room, feeling a bit awkward, I didn't stay long, but I'll never forget what the woman working there told me. This is how I remember it. "Every morning when I start my day reading the Bible Lesson*," she said, "I try to take with me five smooth stones." Before I could ask her what she meant by that, she explained, "I write down and take with me a few passages from *Science and Health* or from the Bible, things that speak to me directly, and I ponder the words throughout the day, holding on to those simple truths as spiritual reinforcements for that particular day." Her face lit up with a smile at this point. "And each time I do that, it changes everything. Healings happen all day long." I thanked her and went on my way.

At the time I didn't think much of it. But it started tugging at me. Having been brought up attending Lutheran Sunday School, I knew I was supposed to know what her reference to "five smooth stones" was, but for the life of me I couldn't remember what it meant. It started to embarrass me a little. I had read the Bible cover to cover a number of times in my life, and especially since I was a preacher's kid, I certainly ought to know what she was talking about. Finally, I looked it up — and of course, there it was: the story of David and Goliath. This Bible story had actually been one of my favorites as a child — but I'd forgotten that David had taken "five smooth stones" with him — I recalled only that he'd knocked that giant down dead with *one* blow. From then on I decided to cherish that tale once again, to study Eddy's writings more closely, and to find out what scientific healing prayer was all about. I will probably never find out who that woman was, but to her I express warm thanks. She planted the seed for this book, pointing me in the right direction.

I am blessed with an exceptionally wonderful husband, David C. Johnson, who graciously and selflessly gave me the space and time I needed to finish this book. So thanks to my dear David, for his patience, good humor, boundless love, and steadfast encouragement. I'm also grateful to our darling daughter Ruby, who with her strength, grace, and joy teaches me something new each day.

I also wish to express gratitude to healer Patricia Tupper Hyatt, CSB, who has helped me shape and grow my healing practice. Extra appreciation goes to my parents and to my husband, who provided significant financial resources as well as moral support. If it weren't for their extraordinary generosity, this book would not be a reality.

The following very special people gave me valuable feedback or advice about the book for which I continue to be grateful: Sarah Cribb; A. B. Curtiss; my brother, Aaron Hunt; Elaine Hunt Fielder; Emily Folmar; David, John, and Krista Holmstrom; my parents J. Richard Hunt and Marj Hunt; Stephen Kiesling; Beca Lewis; Lysa McDowell; Madelon Miles; Ineke Murakami; Ruthie Painter; James Twyman; Katie Tyndall; Debra Valencia; Diana Van Vleck; David Walter; Julie Ward; Deb Wilson; and Devorah Gordon Zaslow. Last, but not least, huge thanks go to David Zaslow, my *rebbe* and friend who finally brought this book to print when no one else would.

Janis Hunt Johnson
Medford, Oregon, 2008

* In the Christian Science tradition there is a weekly *Bible Lesson* containing readings from the Bible and from Mary Baker Eddy's seminal work, *Science and Health*. Each week's citations comprise the Sunday sermon, which is read aloud by two Readers at all Christian Science churches worldwide.

ABOUT THE AUTHOR

Janis Hunt Johnson began the study of spiritual healing in 1991 after she experienced a dramatic physical healing through prayer alone. In 1995 she completed formal Christian Science instruction in Columbia, South Carolina, and attends annual refresher courses since then. She has worked as a professional writer and editor since 1983, and has run her own business as Managing Editor of Ask Janis Editorial & Rewrite Services since 1994. She graduated with a BA in English and Art History from Indiana University (Bloomington) in 1982, and earned an MLS degree there the following year, working as a librarian at the Art Institute of Chicago while launching her freelance career. For nearly a decade she also moonlighted as a singer/songwriter/guitarist and recording artist in Chicago and Los Angeles — with three original albums and an EP to her credit, along with local and national airplay.

Janis now lives with her husband David and young daughter Ruby in Southern Oregon. She loves world travel, camping, movies, cooking, and singing. She is currently learning Hebrew, and studies Torah and Talmud with Jewish Renewal Rabbi David Zaslow. She has published feature articles on the universality of practical spirituality since 1997 for such publications as www.spirituality.com and *The Christian Science Monitor*. *Five Smooth Stones* is her first book.

Janis offers a private healing practice in Southern Oregon. Her goal is to serve, educate, and heal others through the continued study and practical application of scientific prayer in everyday life. Anyone seeking healing of any problem — physical, mental, emotional, financial, etc. — can contact Janis for treatment by visiting her Website at www.csrenewal.com, or calling 971/285-7913. (Outside of Oregon call 888/709-9295. A meeting in person is possible by appointment, but not necessary; distance has no bearing on the effectiveness of healing treatment.)

cs renewal

CS Renewal is an imprint of The Wisdom Exchange, an ecumenical publishing company in Ashland, Oregon founded by Rabbi David Zaslow.

WE! THE WISDOM EXCHANGE
...STANDING IN UNITY AT THE CUTTING EDGE
OF RENEWAL IN SPIRITUAL PRACTICE.